Susan Richards

Poetry. Wayside Thoughts.

A collection of poems on various subjects, sacred, special, and tributary, with some

few thoughts in prose

Susan Richards

Poetry. Wayside Thoughts.
A collection of poems on various subjects, sacred, special, and tributary, with some few thoughts in prose

ISBN/EAN: 9783337373696

Printed in Europe, USA, Canada, Australia, Japan

Cover: Foto ©Thomas Meinert / pixelio.de

More available books at **www.hansebooks.com**

POETRY.

WAYSIDE ·THOUGHTS,

A COLLECTION OF POEMS ON VARIOUS SUBJECTS,

SACRED, SPECIAL,

AND

TRIBUTARY.

WITH SOME FEW THOUGHTS IN PROSE.

———

BY

MRS. SUSAN RICHARDS,

ALAMEDA, CAL.

.

PACIFIC PRESS
TWELFTH AND CAS
529 COMMER

Dedicatory.

———

THIS Little Book is affectionately dedicated
to my dearly beloved children, at whose desire it
is published, and to whom I trust it will prove a source
of sweet remembrances when the writer shall have
passed into the " Land beyond the River."

THE AUTHOR.

CONTENTS.

CONTENTS.

CONTENTS.

RELIGIOUS POEMS.

THE LOVE OF THE SAVIOUR.

SOME write of the love of the youth and the maiden;
With books on the subject our shelves are all laden;
Some write upon friendship, one man for another;
A few have attempted the love of a mother;
I will write of a love that does all these excel;
'Tis the love of the Saviour. Ah, who can it tell!

It dawned in the garden, but the morning was far;
It beamed on for ages, like a glimmering star,
From Eden to Bethlehem, tho' dim was the light,
'Til it burst on the shepherds in glory at night.
Then it brought down from Heaven the angelic throng,
And it caused them to sing that beautiful song.

It was love sent the star that directed the road
Which led right to the dear little stranger's abode.
There he lay in the manger—so peaceful, so sweet,
While the sages brought presents, and laid at his feet.
Oh, the love of the Saviour! Ah, see where it smiled
In the soul-speaking eyes of that beautiful child!

2

In the days of his childhood, the home of his youth,
How pure his behavior, full of wisdom and truth!
And when grown up a man full of sorrows he stood;
Love to all was his labor, his meat to do good;
To the sad and the poor, and the hearts that were broke,
Oh, the beautiful words he in tenderness spoke!

'Twas privation and poverty, malice, distress
He received from their hands whom he came to bless;
Yet how softly he walked over life's thorny path!
Who can point out a fault from his birth to his death?
He gave rest to the weary, sweet peace from on high,
But his own aching head he had no place to lie.

When he sweat in the garden in anguish and woe,
'Twas an angel hand wiped the big drops from his brow,
For the few that did love him had laid down to rest,
And forgotten their Master's most touching request.
Their eyes, they were heavy, soon they fell fast asleep,
And there left him in silence to watch and to weep.

His foes took him to judgment, to torture, to death,
But no word of reproach escaped from his breath.
Oh, that deep, heavy darkness, without a relief!
Yet, in midst of it all, he could pardon the thief.
Ah, say, is it nothing, Oh, all ye who pass by,
That so lovely a being should suffer and die?

The love of the Saviour! Soon it burst from the grave,
Triumphant in power, and almighty to save,
Met the sorrowing few as in sadness they rove,
Gave them their commission and then went up above,
Sent the Comforter down, who he said should descend,
And promised to be with his church to the end.

The love of the Saviour! It is life from the dead;
'Tis a well-spring of water, 'tis heavenly bread;
'Tis a fountain of joy, to cheer life's saddest hours,
And make of a desert a garden of flowers;
'Tis a bright ray of sunshine o'er earth's darkest path;
'Tis a rod and a staff in the valley of death.

The love of the Saviour! 'Tis a song in the night;
'Tis a river of peace, 'tis a sea of delight;
The key-note of the tunes sung by heavenly choirs
To the golden harp music and seraphic lyres.
But oh! sweeter than this, 'tis the song of the blest;
Yes, the beautiful song of the weary at rest.

The love of the Saviour! Oh, the theme is too high;
O'erwhelmed with its greatness, my pen I lay by.
These few thoughts my poor heart hath set all a-glow.
Oh, I wish all the world that same rapture might know!
'Tis eternity's work; nor too long will it prove
For all his redeemed ones to tell of his love.

The love of the Saviour! Dear friend, have you found it?
Then to sinners around go tell all about it.
Go tell it the prayerless, the thoughtless, the gay;
Ah, yes, tell it those who are passing away.
Both at home and abroad, and when by the way-side,
Oh, remember the love of the once crucified.

CONFIDENCE.

" Casting all your care upon him, for he careth for you." I Peter 5:7.

'TIS sweet to be alone with God
   In sorrows tearful hour,
Lie all resigned beneath his rod,
   Trust his love and power.

'Tis sweet to tell him every grief,
   Although in broken speech,
For those deep wounds he'll find relief
   No other hand can reach.

'Tis sweet to take him all my care
   When no one else is by,
No stranger eye to watch the tear,
   No ear to catch the sigh.

'Tis sweet when bowed beneath a cross,
   Whose weight is agony,
As head and heart with anguish toss,
   To know he cares for me.

Sweet, when the waves of trouble roll,
    And adverse winds blow chill,
To lean on him my fainting soul,
    And know the storm he'll still.

Sweet as the billows o'er me sweep,
    And threaten to o'erwhelm,
To know that naught can wreck the ship
    With Jesus at the helm.

Sweet, when the clouds have hid my sky
    And covered every star,
To know they're only passing by—
    The silver lining's there.

Sweet, when thorns have pierced my feet
    From off some rugged road,
To know the roughest path I meet
    Will lead to his abode.

Sweet, as the dear ones pass away
    To sleep beneath the sod,
To know, though here awhile I stay,
    I'll find them safe with God.

Sweet, as life's toiling day moves on,
  And brings approaching night,
To know, as sinks my setting sun,
  At eve it shall be light.

Sweet, as the vale of death appears,
  To meet that cheering ray,
And know, as drops the parting tears,
  He'll wipe them all away.

Sweet, as I near the Jordan's stream,
  To know he'll bear me o'er,
And take me home to dwell with him
  Forever, evermore.

SPEAK SOFTLY.

"A soft answer turneth away wrath." Prov. 15: 1.   "Pleasant words are as a honey-
comb, sweet to the soul, and health to the bones."   Prov. 16: 24.

SPEAK softly, mother, to thy child;
   'Twill make it love thy name;
Teach it in accents meek and mild;
   'Twill learn to speak the same.

Speak softly, father, to thy son,
   With boyish spirits gay,
And your commands will then be done;
   He'll cheerfully obey.

Speak softly, husband, to thy wife;
   Grieve not her gentle breast;
To thee she gave herself for life,
   Make not that life unblest.

Speak softly, wife, to him who toils
   Thy comforts to provide,
And meet him with a face of smiles;
   'Twill keep him by thy side.

Speak softly to the youthful throng;
   Crosses enough they'll meet;
Who knows what storms are o'er them hung
   In future days to beat.

Speak softly to the wearied one,
    The aged, careworn breast;
The old folks' work will soon be done,
    Soothe then, their path to rest.

Speak softly in the stranger's ear;
    In sadness he may roam,
Perhaps in loneliness and tears;
    Oh, make him feel at home.

Speak softly to thy fellow-man;
    His wrath 'twill turn away;
Make peace on earth where'er you can,
    For short may be your stay.

Speak softly to the troubled mind;
    Bind up the broken heart;
To poor and needy, lame and blind,
    Act well a neighbor's part.

Speak softly; 'tis a rugged road,
    At best we travel in;
Kindness lightens many a load,
    And cannot yield a pain.

Speak softly; 'tis an easy thing,
    'Twill never cost a tear;
For happiness kind words will bring,
    And help to soothe our care.

Then let us kindly speak and smile
While here on earth we rove;
'Twill give us in this world of toil
A taste of Heaven above.

———

BE YE ALSO READY.

Matthew 24:44.

OH, be ready for death, for you know not the day
The messenger angel may come!
Oh, be ready for death, for you know not the way
You shall pass to your final home!

He may come at the dawn of the morning light,
Or the heat of the noontide hour;
In the calmness of eve, or the stillness of night,
He may enter your chamber door.

He may come as you walk amid fragrant bowers,
With music of birds in your ear;
He may come in the breeze, the plants, or the flowers,
Or the fruit, delicious and rare.

He may come on the hill-top, or down in the dell,
  At the foot of some lonely tree,
With no one to say a last loving farewell—
  No eye but the Master's to see.

He may come to sweet home, and you on your pillow
  Unconsciously sleeping in peace;
He may come when you're far away on the billow
  Mid the noise of the raging seas.

He may come in the fire; he may come in the storm;
  Terrific the summons may be.
Or perhaps in slow fever consuming your form
  You shall his pale countenance see.

He may come in a whirlwind, or earthquake shock
  Each face white with terror appears;
He may come in the wreck of a ship on a rock,
  And you sink amid crying and tears.

He may come in the crash of a passenger train,
  Or fall from a startled horse.
An explosion of powder, or bursting of steam,
  May leave you a frightful corpse.

He may come in the streets of your own native land,
  As you mix with the good and brave;
He may come far away on some lone, distant strand,
  And you lie in a stranger's grave.

He may come in a draught from a poisoned cup,
   Or blow from assassin's knife;
Or disease may your reason so sadly break up
   That your own hand may end your life.

He may come in the bustle and business of life,
   To the office, the desk, the store;
And, alas! he may come in some sad scene of strife,
   And kindly you'll never speak more.

He may come without warning, suffering, or pain—
   In a second pulsation may cease;
He may come in anguish or delirium of brain,
   Or tedious, lingering disease.

He may come to the church on a bright Sabbath-day,
   Or the week's sweet hour of prayer;
He may come to the ball-room, the opera, the play;
   How would you like to meet him there?

He may come in a moment, a whisper, a breath,
   Who can tell when the time shall be?
Oh, then let us be ready, dear reader, for death!
   He *will come* to *you* and to *me*.

THE HEART.

" 'The heart knoweth its own bitterness, and a stranger doth not intermeddle with its joy."
Proverbs 14: 10.

THE heart has sorrows of its own,
And grief to other hearts unknown,
Though oft', mid pleasure's countless wiles,
They hide beneath a face of smiles.

I've seen the young and lovely fair
The gayest of the gay appear,
But deepest anguish all the while
Lay underneath each dimpled smile.

I've marked the noble, manly youth,
Whose forehead spoke of love and truth,
His wounded heart strive to beguile,
And cover sorrows with a smile.

I've noticed too the man of care
Try hard a pleasant look to wear;
Known woman, in domestic toil,
Hide bitter woe beneath a smile.

Oh, envy not the smiling face!
If you each burning thought could trace,
The sweetest smiles which some employ
Would prove the mockery of joy.

Smiles meant to hide a heart of gloom
Are like the flowers above the tomb;
Like beauteous roses, budding fair
And blooming o'er the sepulcher.

The heart alone its grief can tell,
Nor can the tongue its joys reveal;
For, buried from the world unknown,
The heart hath treasures all its own.

To think of those on earth we love,
Or those who dwell in Heaven above,
Of dear one's absent, friends departed,
Will often soothe the broken-hearted.

Thoughts of the heart, how dear they are!
The unheard sigh, the unseen tear,
The secret wish, the silent prayer—
No stranger eye intrudeth there. .

But it is well to wear a smile;
Gloom will no breaking heart beguile;
'Tis kindly looks and words of love
That can to woe a solace prove.

The worldling in his gayest hours
Hides bitterness beneath the flowers;
The Christian in his darkest night
Hath joys which make his pathway light.

The heart hath sorrows of its own,
And joys to other hearts unknown;
But One alone can it unseal,
And He the broken heart will heal.

———

THE PEACE OF JESUS.

"Peace I leave with you, my peace I give unto you." John 14: 27.

THE peace of Jesus, pledge of love,
  To weary pilgrims given,
Sweet foretaste of the rest above,
  Rest of saints in Heaven!

The peace of Jesus, oh, how high
  It makes the spirit soar,
And all the storms of earth defy,
  Though loud the tempest roar!

The peace of Jesus, oh, how deep,
  No tongue or pen can tell !
When o'er the soul the billows sweep,
  It still can say, All's well.

The peace of Jesus, oh, how strong,
  The weak frame to sustain;
Smooth the rough path we walk along,
  And take away each pain !

The peace of Jesus, oh, how kind !
  It lightens every care;
The broken spirit it doth bind,
  And wipe the mourner's tear.

The peace of Jesus, oh, how calm
  The heart that knows its power !
For every wound it has a balm,
  And cheers each lonely hour.

The peace of Jesus, oh, how still
  When all the world is noise !
No thief the precious gem can steal;
  No foe disturb its joys.

The peace of Jesus, oh, how pure !
  No shade of ruffled breath—
Gentle, serene, and firm, and sure,
  And faithful unto death.

The peace of Jesus, oh, how sweet
   Down in the heart's deep core!
Dear Saviour, give me this complete,
   I'll want for nothing more!

The peace of Jesus, joy sublime!
   If this dwell in my breast,
'Twill bear me o'er the seas of time
   To my eternal rest.

THE BETTER LAND.

" I would not live alway."   Job 7: 16.

I WOULD not live alway
   Where grief rends the heart,
Where fond hopes fly away,
   And comforts depart.

I would not live alway
   Where care casts us down,
Where friends smile to-day,
   And to-morrow will frown.

I would not live alway
  Where tears dim the eye,
Where health will decay,
  And loved ones must die.

There's a land of pure love
  Where all sorrow shall cease;
There are mansions above,
  And a sweet home of peace.

There's the beautiful city
  With streets of pure gold;
There's rest for the weary
  In its glittering fold.

There's the beautiful river
  With bright silver spray,
Making glad forever
  The fair realms of day.

There's the beautiful flowers
  That perennial bloom
In the fragrant bowers
  Of the saints' happy home.

There are beautiful crowns
  Set with diamonds bright,
And there's emerald thrones
  For the robed in white.

There's the beautiful lion,
 Still more beautiful lamb—
He who brought us to Zion,
 The Redeemer his name.

There's the beautiful throne
 With its rainbow of gems,
And there sits on it One
 Who is brighter than them.

'Tis our Heavenly Father,
 Our Judge reconciled,
And around him shall gather
 Each dearly loved child.

There's the loved and the lost
 Of the long, long ago—
Oh, the tears that it cost
 To lay them down low!

There's the dear little friend
 Of our childhood hours,
Who away from us went
 As we ran in the flowers.

There's the loved of our youth,
 The young heart's dearest gem.
Oh, the beautiful truth,
 We shall see them again!

There's our dear little buds,
   And sweet blossoms so fair;
And we've early ripe fruits
   Fondly clustering there.

There's companions in toil,
   Gone away from our side,
Who have left us awhile
   Upon life's stormy tide.

In that multitude throng
   Sainted mothers appear.
Hark! that beautiful song!
   Don't you wish you were there

To join in the chorus
   Of the soul-thrilling strain,
Hallelujah to Jesus!
   Praise the Lamb that was slain!

I would not stay below
   If my choice were given.
No! my soul pants to know
   The sweet rest of Heaven.

THE TREE OF LIFE.

Revelation 22: 2.

THE tree of life stands in the city of God;
    Twelve manner of fruits it doth bear;
Its evergreen leaves, when scattered abroad,
    For healing the nations appear.

Redeemed ones feast on that wonderful tree,
    And dwell in its shade over there;
But it yieldeth its fruit for you and for me
    Each month of our pilgrimage year.

There is fruit for the month of repentance,
    When with tears the eyes overflow;
And there's fruit for the month of acceptance,
    When pardon the spirit doth know.

There is fruit for the month of temptation,
    When faith bids the tempter to cease;
And there's fruit for the month of salvation—
    Constant trust, which bringeth forth peace.

There is fruit for the months of trouble and grief,
    .Months of conflict, trial, and care,
When the joy of the Lord giveth glad relief,
    And strength every burden to bear.

Fruit for the months of affliction and sorrow.
  Yes; there's comfort for every breath.
Each sweet promise tells of a brighter morrow—
  Blessed rest, in the month of death.

Oh, those fruits for the soul, of pardon, and peace,
  Faith, hope, and a sanctified love,
Courage, patience, trust, joy, rest, comfort, and bliss
  From that beautiful tree up above!

The yield of this glorious tree cannot fail;
  No worm ever gnaws at its root;
No blighting storms over that land can prevail,
  To wither its life-giving fruit.

Oh, wonderful tree in the city of love!
  Whenever I'm weary, distrest,
My soul takes its wing, and flies up above,
  Beneath its wide branches to rest.

I gaze on its beauty; I eat of its fruit;
  And in its rich foliage I see,
Clustering together, a little white group,
  Who are waiting up there for me.

Dear Saviour, whenever the time shall come
  Thou sendest a message for me,
Oh, give me to rest in a sweet, sweet home,
  Just under that beautiful tree!

MY TIMES ARE IN THY HAND.

" My times are in thy hand." Psalms. 31 :15.

AH, yes; my times are in thy hand;
  What if it were not so?
Could I my path through life command,
  I wonder where I'd go.

What if the task were given to me
  My own fate to indite,
To rule and shape my destiny;
  I wonder what I'd write.

Would I possess unbounded wealth
  And own a large estate?
Enjoy uninterrupted health?
  Rank with the wise and great?

Or would I have a sweet, sweet home,
  Peaceful as Eden's bowers, ·
Where withering storms could never come
  To blight my cherished flowers?

I wonder if I'd put down cares,
 And aught of sorrow know;
Or, would I leave out toil and tears,
 With every shade of woe?

I wonder what I'd say of death—
 Where, when, and at what age
Would I resign this fleeting breath?
 Ah! what about that page?

Oh, 'twere a task too deep, too high
 For such an arm as mine!
To rule one human destiny
 The hand must be divine.

Ah, yes; my times are in His hand.
 Amen! so let it be.
My home is in the better land,
 To that He leadeth me.

THE BEAUTIFUL LAND.

How I love sometimes up the mountain to climb,
   And ascend from this valley of tears,
A moment to gaze on the beautiful clime
   Where my soul shall be free from its cares!

I stand on the top of the evergreen hills
   That o'erlook the celestial bowers;
I sit down by the side of the gentle rills
   That water the beautiful flowers.

I watch the bright seraphim shade with his wing
   His shining face, as he nears the throne;
I hear the sweet songs angel choristers sing
   Of glory, glory to God alone.

But far sweeter to me are the strains that rise
   From the ransomed, the glorified throng,
Whose millions of voices re-echo the skies
   With the swell of their beautiful song.

'Mid the white groups I see on each golden steep,
   Are the loved of the long, long ago,
And the dear little darlings I've laid down to sleep
   'Neath the clods of the valley below.

But there's One above all on whom my glad eye
    In fond rapture forever could gaze,
Great center of every attraction on high,
    The one glorious object of praise.

Jesus, the Master! his presence makes Heaven;
    'Tis his love is the key to their bliss;
He washed their robes white; their sins he's forgiven,
    And prepared them a mansion of peace.

His beautiful smile there's no pencil can paint;
    Its radiance transcends mortal skill;
The most brilliant touch of the artist is faint,
    And the poet's pen too must be still.

I cannot stay long to behold that abode,
    For the duties of life will be prest;
But I run up the hill by the side of the road,
    Just to look at my beautiful rest.

'Tis a soul-thrilling sight, that land of delight;
    As I gaze, down my cheek rolls a tear;
Then I hear a sweet whisper: Fight the good fight,
    And you too—by and by—shall be there.

So I come down again to this region of strife,
    For a little while longer to roam.
When I've done with the toil and turmoil of life,
    I shall go to my beautiful home.

THOUGHTS ON DEATH.

I'D like to die at close of day,
  When all the world is still,
Just as the setting sun's last ray
  Goes down behind the hill.

I'd like to die at evening hour,
  When nature's hushed to rest,
When tired insects seek their bower,
  And weary birds their nest.

I'd like at even-tide to stand
  Close to the Jordan's stream,
And cross to Canaan's happy land,
  By moonlight's silvery beam.

I'd like to die in sweetest peace
  With all on earth below,
That not one thought may mar my bliss
  In the Heav'n, to which I go.

I'd like to know my work was done
  Ere the last hour draws nigh;
I'd like to have, when death shall come,
  Nothing to do but die.

I'd like no crowd around my bed,
　No whispers in my ear,
But one lov'd hand to raise my head,
　Or wipe the latest tear.

I'd like my friends aside to pray,
　Silent, with hearts sincere,
That while in death's dark vale I stay
　No evil I might fear.

I'd like to die in lively faith,
　Trusting in Jesus' blood,
That blood which takes the sting from death,
　And reconciles to God.

I'd like to have my vision clear,
　My hope serene and bright,
To see the promised land appear,
　The haven, full in sight.

Ah, yes; thus I would like to die!
　But, if it may not be,
If o'er my head the waves run high,
　And darkness trouble me,

Dear Saviour, while the billows roll,
　And angry tempests roar,
Do thou but meet my fainting soul;
　I will not ask for more.

If peacefully I shall not die,
   Nor glimpse of glory see,
Oh, let me know that thou art by!
   The rest I'll leave to thee.

THE HEAVENLY INHERITANCE.

THERE'S a beautiful land in the realms of bliss,
Far from all the toil and the troubles of this;
The fields are all green, and the trees ever bloom;
The flowers never fade, nor lose their perfume.
There's a sweet, sweet home in that far-off land,
Where there's naught to divide the family band,
Where sorrow and sighing forever shall flee—
That beautiful home, faithful Christian's for thee.

There's a beautiful robe made of spotless white—
'Tis an every-day dress in that land of light;
There's a palm of victory, a harp of gold,
And a song of love that can never be told;
There's a seat on the throne, and bright starry crown
For him who the name of conqueror shall own.
Rest for the weary, ah, how sweet it will be!
That beautiful rest, faithful Christian's for thee.

How many there are who their Saviour confess!
Very loudly they talk and sing of his grace,
But they walk so unsteady, stumble and fall,
They'll be but just saved—if they're saved at all.
Some will tell us they love at all times to pray—
Yet try from all work to keep out of the way.
They are walking to Heaven at a slow peaceful rate,
Content if they only get in at the gate.

But that will not do for this spirit of mine.
No; I want like a star in glory to shine.
I must have that home of transporting delight;
I must walk those fields with my Saviour, in white;
I must move in the midst of that radiant throng;
I want to sing with them that beautiful song;
I must drink from the fount in that world of bliss,
Whose streams have so often refreshed me in this.

I'll not go alone to the mansion I own;
I must have the dear ones now around the hearth-stone;
I'll take loved friends below to that place so fair;
I'll ask strangers to go, for they're welcome there;
I must have some bright gems to put in my crown;
I must try to get near to my Father's throne.
Just inside the pearly gate won't do for me—
All the fullness of joy my portion must be.

Come ye, who would shine in that heavenly land,
Let us up and be doing, the night is at hand;
We must work to-day in the light of the sun,
We shall mourn if it sets ere our task is done.
There are souls to seek, or they'll languish and die;
There are kind words to speak, and sad tears to dry;
Lead sinners to Jesus, oh, labor of love!
How 'twill sweeten the rest that awaits us above!

THE WHISPERER.

"A whisperer separateth chief friends." Proverbs 16:28.

TRUE, O king, it is true, it was true in thy time,
Has been so in all ages, and in every clime,
All ranks and conditions, men of every station,
High and low, rich and poor, throughout every nation,
Illiterate and wise, the rude, gentle, and wild,
From the gray-headed sage to the dear little child,—
All have learned in the school of experience to prove
That a whisperer cutteth the silk cords of love.

In the palace of monarchs, the homes of the great,
The chambers of commerce, and the councils of State,
At the party, the concert, the ball-room, he's found,
But he is not confined to unhallowed ground.

He's in church among those most devout who appear,
And is often the first at the meetings for prayer.
And estrangement and strife and disunion prove
That a whisperer cutteth the sweet bands of love.

Oft the whisperer weareth a smooth face of smiles —
Beware! they are only the false hypocrite's wiles.
Like the spider he weaveth a flattering spell,
Winding up with a promise that you will not tell.
Oh, promise it not, but the slanderer disown!
That must surely be wrong he's afraid to have known.
Alas, sad wounded spirits and broken hearts prove
That a whisperer cutteth the soft cords of love!

Yes; the whisperer has broken many a heart.
He has parted the friends that no tempest could part;
Lent a withering blight o'er life's fairest flowers;
Turned the brightest of sunshine to midnight hours.
There's a venomous shaft in his poisoned breath
That can make a sweet home a dark mansion of death.
Oh, there's millions of hearts in this wide world can prove
That a whisperer cutteth the sweet bands of love!

Ah, don't be a whisperer, my lively young friend,
If you'd have peace and joy all your pathway attend!
But think kindly, speak kindly, where'er you may roam,
And your name shall be sweet when you've gone to your
        home.

Raise the sad, drooping head, wipe the tears as they fall;
Have a warm, friendly hand and a good word for all;
Turn a deaf ear to slander; deceit disapprove;
For a whisperer cutteth the silk cords of love.

But pity the whisperer all ye people who can,
Despised as he is both by God and by man,
By himself when he stops to consider his ways;
Then remorse makes unhappy the rest of his days.
The words he hath spoken he would gladly recall,
For he feels like an object avoided by all.
Oh, 'tis soothing to know that the Scriptures can prove
There's no whisperer found in the Heaven above!

DEAD FLIES.

'Dead flies cause the ointment of the apothecary to send forth a stinking savor; so doth a little folly him that is in reputation for wisdom and honor." Ecclesiastes 10 : 1.

DEAD flies in ointment maketh it foul,
So folly in wise men soileth the soul.
Dirt spots on a dingy old coat don't show,
On new, superfine, their presence you'll know.

4

The man who has gained position and wealth
By honest toil and the blessing of health,
But forgets the friends who helped him when poor,
Has flies in his ointment you may be sure.

The man who puts on religion on Sundays,
But business lies tells freely on Mondays,
Runs deeply in debt, is not true to his word—
The dead flies in his ointment displease the Lord.

The man who boasts his charities world wide,
But can pass a poor man, faint by his side;
All smiles in public, at home cross, unkind—
Dead flies in his ointment very worst kind.

The man who in meeting talks long and loud
Of his own good deeds, to the silent crowd,
Points out others' faults, thanks God he's not so—
Dead flies in Pharisee's ointment, you know.

The man who has always some secret to tell
He's heard about others who don't behave well,
Goes from house to house, dealing slander and news—
Dead flies in the ointment that whisperers use.

The man of good name and fair reputation,
Who thinks there's no harm in a little flirtation,
Twines round a young heart, then the cords coolly sever;
Dead flies in his ointment; they'll stain him forever.

The man who talks of sanctification,
But lives for selfish gratification,
Is grasping for wealth, stoops to anything mean—
Dead flies in his ointment; his hands are not clean.

The pastor who cares for the rich and well-drest,
But neglects the poor, the sick, the distrest,
May preach like a Paul, like an angel may sing—
Dead flies in the ointment; like brass it will ring

But, alas! I confess with sorrow, I own,
That gentlemen use not this ointment alone;
There are beautiful ladies, gentle and wise,
Whose sweetest perfumes are full of dead flies—

Anger, jealousy, malice, vanity, pride,
Idle gossip and slander, with a host beside.
On a pure white dress spots will plainest appear.
Ah! these dead flies cause many a bitter tear.

Who can count their names?   Alas! they are legion.
They spoil our good sense, disgrace our religion.
Oh, who does not long for that beautiful shore
Where folly and flies shall annoy us no more!

THE HIGHER LIFE.

"The secret of the Lord is with them that fear him."   Psalms 25 : 14.

THE Christian has a higher life,
   'Tis hid with Christ in God;
He's passing through a world of strife,
   But lives above the road.

He knows the secret of the Lord,
   That secret, oh, how dear!
There's naught on earth that can afford
   Such bliss the soul to cheer.

He talks with Jesus at the ray
   Of morn's first dawning light;
He walks with Jesus all the day,
   And rests with him at night.

He lives in Heaven all the while;
   He has a mansion fair;
And, though mid earthly care and toil,
   He lays up treasure there.

The spirit doth his grace impart,
  And holy fire reveal;
And Jesus on his inmost heart
  Does his own image seal.

He'll never say in accents vain,
  I holier am than thou;
But holiness in letters plain
  Is written on his brow.

While he enjoys the rest of faith,
  His heart and hands are clean;
No word impure will soil his breath,
  And he'll do nothing mean.

In all his dealings he'll be just,
  The path of right pursue.
Faithful he'll prove to every trust,
  And what he says will do.

He'll live for God, where'er he roves,
  And make his mercy known;
Tell sinners of a Saviour's love,
  And lead the wanderer home.

He'll kindly raise the drooping head
  That in his path may lie,
And gently smooth the dying bed—
  The mourner's tear-drops dry.

He'll scatter round a cheerful beam
    Where gloomy weeds have grown,
And take to Heaven many a gem
    To deck the Saviour's crown.

The world may look with cold disdain
    Upon his upright walk;
Slanderers try his name to stain—
    He'll overcome the talk.

The thunder o'er his head may roll,
    The vivid lightning flash;
The earth may shake from pole to pole—
    He'll calmly stand the crash.

When clouds of sorrow shade his sky,
    And grief his soul has crash'd,
He thinks of his sweet home on high,
    And every sigh is hush'd.

And when for him the angels wait,
    His work will all be done;
They'll bear him through the pearly gate,
    Up to his Father's throne.

He'll have the name within the stone;
    And spotless robe so fair;
He'll have the palm, the harp, the crown,
    And dwell forever there.

THE SECRET PLACE.

" He that dwelleth in the secret place of the Most High shall abide under the shadow of the Almighty." Psalms 91:1.

THE secret place, Oh, sacred spot!
My arbor, where the world comes not;
My soul's sweet rest, full and complete;
The garden where my God I meet.
Whene'er bowed down with grief and care,
I hide in his pavilion there.

The secret place, no stranger ear
Can listen to my humble prayer;
The secret place, no eye can see
My God descend and talk with me.
Dear Father, to this spot I cling,
Under the shadow of thy wing.

The secret place of the Most High,
No envious feet are passing by.
Turmoil and strife may rage around,
They cannot touch my hallowed ground.
Father, I'll come, whate'er betide,
In this dear spot my soul to hide.

The secret place, so pure, so bright,
Here I gain strength to meet the fight;
Tempest may rise and storms may come,
They only drive me nearer home.
My Father, to this spot I cling,
Under the shadow of thy wing.

The secret place, Oh, blessed spot!
My sheltering rock, my mountain-top,
From whence I view the streets of gold,
And catch a glimpse of bliss untold;
My Beulah Land on which I stand,
Hid in the hollow of His hand.

The secret place, here I must dwell;
With love and joy my heart doth swell.
Here let my latest sun go down,
'Neath golden light from off thy throne.
Dear Father, still just here I'll cling,
Under the shadow of thy wing.

GOLDEN APPLES.

"A word fitly spoken is like apples of gold in pictures of silver."   Proverbs 25:11.

TENDER words spoken
To hearts that are broken
Are surely the words the wise man hath named;
Their worth is untold.
They are apples of gold—
Those who speak them are pictures in which they're
framed.

Speak lovingly then
To the children of men.
Ah! why should life's pathway be shaded with gloom?
Husbands, speak tenderly,
Wives, ever so gently,
Keep apples of gold framed in silver at home.

And, mother, speak mild
To the dear little child,
For it may not with you have long to remain.
Keep love in the fold,
'Tis an apple of gold,
And you are the silver in which it is framed.

Speak kind to the young,
For it will not be long
Ere, out in the world, by rough words they'll be pained.
Tell love's story old;
Give them apples of gold;
They'll love the bright pictures in which they are
framed.

Softly speak to the lost,
On sin's tempest tossed,
And lift up the fallen, no matter how low.
Better than money
And sweeter than honey
Are apples of gold framed in silver aglow.

Soothe the wounded heart,
It will best heal the smart.
Speak sweet words of love to cheer life's saddest hours;
'Twill comfort the weary,
Brighten the dreary—
They are apples of gold set in silver flowers.

Bring wanderers home,
That in sorrow now roam.
Kind words fitly spoken, the wise man hath well named.
Their worth can't be told,
They are apples of gold,
And you are the pictures in which they are framed.

THE WORLD.

THE young heart views the world an enchanting scene,
  With fairy lights all of a glow;
Thinks all is sweet peace that is looking serene,
  And gold that is glittering so.

They build beautiful castles high in the air,
  And furnish with pleasure and joy,
Never thinking the skies are not always fair,
  Or that winds their house may destroy.

They lay their bright plans for a future career,
  Launch ships on a fanciful sea,
And stay not to think that a tempest is near,
  And their vessel a wreck might be.

But we cannot sail long on a calm still tide
  Ere a storm most surely appears--
At first overwhelm'd is the heart's early pride;
  Ah, how warm are our youthful tears!

Our riches take wing, and away goes our wealth,
  And poverty comes with its woe;
Or diseases appear, and we lose our health,
  And then pain and sorrow we know.

There are darling children to suffer and die,
    While parents in agony weep,
And dearly beloved ones to whisper good-bye,
    And part perhaps never to meet.

Death will come to our home and take from our eyes
    Dearest objects of fond delight;
Joy is but a phantom—we chase it, it flies—
    And the world's like a winter's night.

Oh, what could we do were we left in the dark
    With no hope of a future home?
A sad picture of gloom, without one bright spark
    To light up beyond the cold tomb.

But thanks be to God, who gave revelation,
    Blessed book to brighten our path.
Hallelujah to Jesus! who brought us salvation,
    Safe now is the valley of death.

Oh, then lay up stores in that beautiful home,
    Where naught our treasure can sever;
Where care, disappointment, and sorrows ne'er come,
    But joy forever and ever.

THE TREE OF METHODISM.

CENTENARY HYMN.

OH, rally round the good old tree,
  Planted by Wesley's hand;
And let its lofty branches be
  The glory of the land.
He placed it in the fair new soil,
  And wet it with his tears;
To-day we hail it with a smile—
  Growth of a hundred years.

        Then rally round the tree, friends,
        The broad, the noble tree.
        Large let your offerings be, friends,
        On this glad jubilee.

Think of the pious, earnest few,
  Who watched its early growth;
Labor, fatigue, and care they knew,
  But faithful were to truth.
Oh, for their consecrated will,
  Their energetic fire,
Their pure and holy fervent zeal,
  Our own hearts to inspire!

        Then rally round the tree, etc.

What millions now arrayed
  In robes of spotless white,
First met with Jesus 'neath its shade
  In sorrow's weary night!
He knows them all, each one by name,
  With every state and place,
Each spot of earth from whence they came,
  To rest in his embrace.

> Then rally round the tree, etc.

Our Father, we will bless thy name,
  For this our glorious tree.
Oh, help us, Lord, to spread thy fame
  O'er every land and sea!
Oh, send us heavenly showers,
  Spirit of burning love,
Come with thy reviving powers,
  And raise our hearts above.

> Then rally round the tree, etc.

Clear as the sun, with radiance bright,
  Our tree shall ever bloom,
Fair as the moon, whose silver light
  Shines o'er the midnight gloom;

Like one grand army drawn in line,
　　All terrible to foes;
So shall our starry banner shine,
　　Whatever may oppose.

　　　　　Then rally round the tree, etc.

Oh, yes; we'll gather round the tree,　　•
　　Beneath its branches come.
Before the next grand jubilee
　　We shall have reached our home;
We shall with our Redeemer be;
　　He'll wipe off every tear;
But there we'll not forget the tree
　　That gave us shelter here.

　　　　　Then rally round the tree, etc.

All honor to the faithful few
　　Who first did till the land;
And broadcast o'er Columbia threw
　　The seed, with steady hand.
When earth and time have passed away,
　　Rich glory they shall share;
A brilliant crown with dazzling ray,
　　Each on his brow shall wear.

　　　　　Then rally round the tree, etc.

And when we all arrive at home,
 Oh, what a shout we'll raise!
We'll shake the high celestial dome
 With our loud songs of praise;
On Wesley's head we'll put a crown,
 Where million gems shall meet;
And then we'll help him take it down
 To lay at Jesus' feet.

   Then rally round the tree, friends,
   The broad, the noble tree.
   Large let your offerings be, friends,
   On this grand jubilee.

San Francisco, April 23, 1866.

FAREWELL TO LINCOLN.

FAREWELL to thee, Lincoln, true, honest, and brave;
Thou nobly did'st toil thy country to save;
But thy mission is ended; thy work is well done;
The battle is fought, and the victory is won.
Farewell! oh, farewell! thou has left us forever,
But we'll never forget thee—ah, never, no never!

Farewell to thee, Lincoln; we grieve o'er thy doom;
We could wish thou had'st died in the bosom of home,
With loved ones to soothe, altho' broken-hearted,
And say one farewell as thy spirit departed.
Farewell! oh, farewell! thou hast left us forever,
But we'll never forget thee—ah, never, no never!

Farewell to thee, Lincoln; we mourn thy decease,
But rejoice thou did'st see the first dawning of peace;
Like Moses, beheld, from the mount of the blest,
The beautiful land where his people should rest.
Farewell! oh, farewell! thou hast left us forever,
But we'll never forget thee—ah, never, no never!

Farewell to thee, Lincoln; thy death has but sealed
The new laws by which the nation is healed.

The death warrant of slavery lies before God;
It is wrote by thy pen; it is sealed with thy blood.
Farewell! oh, farewell! thou hast left us forever,
But we'll never forget thee—ah, never, no never!

Farewell to thee, Lincoln; Rebellion is dead;
Thou hast crush'd with thy foot the vile monster's head;
Thou hast fought a good fight; thou shalt now wear a
    crown,
And Columbia forever shall chant thy renown.
Farewell! oh, farewell! thou hast left us forever,
But we'll never forget thee—ah, never, no never!

Farewell to thee, Lincoln; perhaps it is best
Thou should'st pass from the valley of conflict to rest;
Thou hast finished the work thou wert called to perform;
Thou hast met every foe, and braved every storm.
Farewell! oh, farewell! thou hast left us forever,
But we'll never forget thee—ah, never, no never!

Farewell to thee, Lincoln; how sweet is thy sleep,
Tho' millions of eyes o'er thy murder will weep!
Thy name is untarnished; thy fame shall be sung
While the world shall endure, and man has a tongue.
Farewell! oh, farewell! thou hast left us forever,
But we'll never forget thee—ah, never, no never!

Farewell to thee, Lincoln; may our Father and God
Still watch o'er the land hallow'd now by thy blood.
Oh yes; he's the God of sweet liberty's home—
He's our refuge and strength, and his kingdom shall
    come.
Farewell! oh, farewell! thou hast left us forever,
But we'll never forget thee—ah, never, no never.

San Francisco, April, 1865.

FAREWELL TO SLAVERY.

FAREWELL to thee, Slavery, a hearty farewell!
There's no sorrow springs up at thy parting knell,
But loud shouts of joy, which shall rise to the skies,
And echo repeat the glad sound as it flies;
For no more shall thy name our bright banner stain—
No, never; oh, never; no never again!

Farewell to thee, Slavery! The sufferer's moan,
The strong man's grief, and the old man's groan,
The poor mother's grief, and the little one's cry
Have pierced the ears of the Lord most high;
And no more shall thy name our bright banner stain—
No, never; oh, never; no never again!

Farewell to thee, Slavery! Our dear ones have fell;
As we call them to mind our beating hearts swell.
Thou hast slain thy ten thousands with bitterest hate,
But the last of thy victims was Lincoln the great;
For no more shall thy name our bright banner stain—
No, never; oh, never; no never again!

Farewell to thee, Slavery! A long list of crime
Shall go with thee down through the annals of time;
And the people unborn shall read the sad woe,
Rejoicing thou'rt gone to the long, long ago.
Oh, no more shall thy name our bright banner stain—
No, never; oh, never; no never again!

Farewell to thee, Slavery! thou curse of the land,
Wiped out by Jehovah's omnipotent hand;
When he whets his glittering sword to slay,
Ah, where is the power his arm can stay?
Oh, no more shall thy name our bright banner stain—
No, never; oh, never; no never again!

Farewell to thee, Slavery! 'Tis a costly sum;
It has taken the light from many a home;
The heart of the nation has bled to kill thee,
But, thanks be to God, all the people are free!
Oh, no more shall thy name our bright banner stain—
No, never; oh, never; no never again!

Farewell to thee, Slavery! It will not be long
Ere the universe round shall repeat the same song;
For the mighty of earth are about to discover
That man shall be man the wide world all over.
Oh, no more shall thy name our bright banner stain—
No, never; oh, never; no never again!

Farewell to thee, Slavery! How sweet on our ear
Will the trumpet of jubilee sound thro' the air;
Oh, Jesus, come quickly; take thy power and reign!
Hark! his chariot wheels are approaching the plain.
Oh, no more shall thy name our bright banner stain—
No, never; oh, never; no never again!

Then farewell to thee, Slavery, a hearty farewell!
There's no sorrow springs up at thy parting knell,
But loud shouts of joy, which shall rise to the skies,
And echo repeat the glad sound as it flies;
For no more shall thy name our bright banner stain—
No, never; oh, never; no never again!

THE RAINBOW.

JULY 3, 1865.

OH, say, did you see that beautiful bow
  In the clouds of the evening sky?
'Twas a grand arch of triumph, arose up to show
  That Heaven partook of our joy.

Yes; that beautiful bow, with its radiant glow,
  Was a touch of the Master's hand;
And it gracefully rose, a smile to bestow
  On the grateful joy of the land.

'Twas our Father's bow, full of promise and hope,
  Sweet sign of approval and love;
The floods of deep waters have just been dried up—
  There is rest for the weary dove.

And that brilliant arch was a glorious dispatch
  From the Ruler of earth and sky:
A new covenant to-day I make with all flesh
  That liberty never shall die.

There are storms yet to come, deep floods to arise,
  And many dark systems to fall;
But behold! I have set my bow in the skies,
  A pledge I will bring you through all.

Our Father, we thank thee, with hearts lifted up,
    For the joy thou hast given below;
And if ever our spirits should falter or drop,
    We'll think of that beautiful bow.

That jubilee bow would have been out of place,
    In the calm of the midsummer sky,
If it had not appeared, our triumphs to grace,
    On the eve of the Fourth of July.

San Francisco, July 7, 1865.

———

JULY FOURTH RECITATION.

[For boy or girl.]

ALL hail to the day of our country's birth,
Most glorious of all the nations of earth;
Our goddess of freedom proudly doth stand,
With a home for oppressed ones from every land.

    Then raise the banner high
      O'er city, hill, and plain;
    The brightest flag beneath the sky,
      It waves without a stain.

All hail to the memory of the mighty men,
Who did the Declaration paper pen;
Yes, let their names ring out from shore to shore,
Until nations and time shall be no more.

All hail to George Washington's glorious name!
All hail to Lincoln, who stands next in fame!
All hail to the men who for liberty bled!
All hail the memory of the mighty dead.

All hail to the land where freedom doth rule—
The land of Bibles, of college, and school;
There's no dark spot on our banner so fair,
High let it wave, fling it out on the air.

All hail! above all to our Father in Heaven,
Who to us this beautiful land hath given;
With loud grateful songs let our voices now raise
Till the hills shall re-echo the notes of praise.

Then raise the banner high
O'er city, hill, and plain;
The brightest flag beneath the sky,
It waves without a stain.

GRANDMA'S CHRISTMAS,

AND

OTHER PIECES.

GRANDMA'S CHRISTMAS.

IS Christmas; grandma sits in her easy chair by the fireside; there is company in the parlor and company in the nursery; a large Christmas tree in the sitting-room, all aglow with its variegated lights, every branch laden with presents from Santa Claus,—presents for papa; presents for mamma; presents for every child, even baby; presents too for the company; last, but not least, many a gift of love for grandma. She has passed a very pleasant day, conversed cheerfully with the company, laughed with the children in their merriment, listened to their sweet songs of good-will and peace, and now she has gone to her own room to keep Christmas quietly by herself.

The old live in the past, and so grandma has scarcely sat down ere she has gone back to the days of her childhood in the old home far, far away. For aught she knows there may not be one s tone left upon another of that place so dear to her memory; but there it is with its large rooms and old-fash ioned fire-places, large fires too, for grandma's home was in a climate where frost and snow are frequent accompaniments to Christmas festivities; and there is father and mother busy looking after the Christmas provisions,—geese, turkeys, or roast beef, and the never-to-be-forgotten plum pudding; and there is brother Richard, and James, and David, and Jonathan, sister Rachel, and Ruth, and Nancy, and herself busily trimming up the house with holly, every corner, every window, every looking-glass.   How the red berries are dangling over every quaint old picture, every ornament that stands on or hangs over the broad mantel-shelf!   There too is the mistletoe bough, suspended from the hook in the center of the room—one chief source of the evening's amusement.   There was no Christmas tree then, but presents were called Christmas boxes, of which generally there was a bounteous supply; there were merry games for the children, the principal of which was blind-man's-buff, after which they gathered around the cheerful fire, in whose chimney-corner sat another grandma, whose hair seemed to rival the snow in whiteness; and they sang very heartily the carols of the day: "While shepherds watch their flocks by night," "Hark the herald angels sing," etc.; and the dear old grandmother tells them how they used to keep Christmas in her childhood, and tries to sing to them one of the curious carols she used to sing.   Grandma's eyes are wet now as she thinks of the dear old lady who laid her hands upon her. head, and wished her many a " Merry Christmas" and a "Happy New Year."

Happy children! Christmas was then, is now, and ever shall be most emphatically the children's day.   Unclouded by the memories of the past or anxieties for the future, the birthday of the Babe of Bethlehem is to them a source of the purest, brightest joy. But to return to grandma; the scene changes, or rather passes on, for grandma has a panorama to-night. Christmas eves pass, several of them, like the one I have described, until there comes one which has a vacant chair—yes; more than one; grandmother's white head has been laid away, and sister Ruth sleeps by her side, just down beneath the willows; brother Richard, too, has gone to a home of his own, beyond the sea, and childhood's Christmas has passed away forever; the scene moves on—more changes, more empty chairs, and then grandma is in another home, another family circle, of which she is the center. Reuben, the husband of her youth, stands by her side, and there is another Reuben, and Robert, and a little Ruth, and Bennie, and baby May; and they are laughing at the red berries as they help papa dress the pictures, and they are looking for Christmas boxes and Christmas puddings; singing, too, the same carols, playing the same games. Ah! grandma's eyes are wet again now, for that was baby May's only Christmas, and little Bennie's last one; when Christmas came again they were sleeping beneath the snow. Quicker now the scenes pass by—change after change, losses, crosses, disappointments, journeyings, sicknesses, bereavements, and sorrows, until grandma's spring and summer days are past, and she finds herself in the autumn of life in another home, a stranger in a strange land.

Christmas comes; it is not kept just as she had been accustomed to keep it, but it is still the children's day; there are the same sweet songs of good-will and peace; true, there are new carols, new music, and new methods of enjoyment, but it is still the birthday of the Babe of Bethlehem. Year after year passes. Ah! who can tell all that grandma saw in that quiet panorama?

Old age comes at last, and one Christmas eve when Reuben tells her he believes it is his last one. Wife, he says, it will not be long before you will come to me. If you should stay a few more Christmas days, remember, I shall be thinking of you then. I believe they keep Christmas in Heaven. Surely they do; is it not to the Babe of Bethlehem they owe Heaven? I will look for the children and grandchildren up there, and we will be near you if we can.

After his death grandma went to reside with her daughter. A few years had passed by. She had not forgotten his words, and now, as her thoughts had called up the panorama of her life, how they seemed to sound in her ears: I will surely be near you or look at you at Christmas. O Reuben, said she, could I but see you! And then her thoughts took wing, but her eyes were heavy. Soon her head drooped upon her breast, and she found herself standing by the pearly gates of the celestial city. The gate was ajar; she heard music, sweet music; softly she stepped inside; multitudes were passing in white robes, with harps in their hands, and soon these words rose on her ear, "Glory to God in the highest, good-will and peace to man." Oh! thought she, they are keeping Christmas in Heaven. Reuben was right. But how came I here? Why do they not speak to me? for no one seemed to be aware of her presence. She began to look around upon the glory of the place. She saw the splendor of the great white throne, but she turned away, afraid to look up. Oh! she thought, once I was determined to gain a place upon that throne. I wanted the white robe, the new name, the crown of life—all, all I wanted that is promised to those who shall overcome; but now, now the battle is over; the victory is won. Oh! where will He put me? He knows all my weakness, all my unworthiness. Ah yes; He knows it, knows it altogether! I shall be satisfied where-ever He shall place me. But Reuben, where shall I look for Reuben? I always think of him as just down by the crystal stream. He did so love a home by the water-side. And so she moves along through groups of shining ones until she sees, yes, she does see Reuben, and he is by the beautiful river close to the tree of life, standing near a pretty home all surrounded by flowers. Oh, such flowers! Why, there were roses, and lilies, and violets, and an abundance of others that she had never seen anything like, so beautiful. Oh Reuben, she cried, are those flowers for me? but Reuben does not look at her; he is looking very intently at something that seemed to be beneath him. She felt afraid, but was about to speak to him again, when soft, sweet sounds arose upon her ear; she looked up, and lo! a little group of cherubs upon golden wing approached; they were singing; they did not notice her, but drew near to Reuben, and looked down as he did; then they sang again: We are looking at you, mother; we are waiting for you, mother; yes, waiting for you. How her heart beat now! She looks again. Oh, yes! they are mine, mine, she cried. Why, there's Robert, and Lucy, and Charlie, little Bennie, and baby May! Oh, speak to me, speak to me! Why do you not look at me? Then a gentle voice at her side said, They do not see you, grandma; they are looking at you, but not here; you are not visible here; you are only here in thought. Reuben is looking at you down yonder in your chair by the fireside; your mind was upon him, and I have given you a sight of him and your future home. Go back now; soon you shall come, and they shall see you here. She looked at the speaker. Ah! it needed no words to tell her who it was. She saw Him whom her soul loved, who was to her the chief among ten thousand, the one altogether lovely—He who was the Babe of Bethlehem, the guide of her youth, the friend of her riper years, and the staff of her old age. Full of emotion, she was about to cast herself at his feet, but the excitement caused her to awake. Oh, she cried, it was a dream then, but what a beautiful dream! Why, they are keeping Christmas in Heaven! Yes, oh yes; keeping Christmas in Heaven! Blessed grandma, who can tell when the bells ring out Christmas again but you too may be keeping it in Heaven.

CHRISTMAS.

"GOOD-WILL AND PEACE."

SWEET song of the angels, when they came down to earth
The glad tidings to bring of Immanuel's birth!
In the stillness of night it rang o'er the plains,
While woods, hills, and valleys re-echoed the strains.
'Twas good-will and peace, sang the heavenly throng,
And to-day we repeat that beautiful song.

'Twas good-will and peace to the shepherds came greeting,
And told where the infant Redeemer was sleeping;
It brought the wise men with their gifts from afar,
Guided safe by the rays of Bethlehem's star;
Good-will and peace! ah, how sweetly it smiled
In the lovely face of that beautiful child!

6

There was good-will and peace in his every breath,
Through his life of sorrow, suffering, and death;
Yes, good-will and peace when the blood trickled down
From the piercing points of his thorny crown;
Good-will in the garden, bent in agony low,
When an angel hand wiped the sweat from his brow;

Good-will as he hung upon Calvary's tree,
And purchased salvation for you and for me;
Good-will when he rose and ascended to Heaven;
Good-will and peace to humanity given.
Sweet song of the angels, they brought it to men,
But redeemed ones have sung it ever since then!

Oh, could we but know how they sing it above
When Christmas comes with its memories of love,
Our dear ones, whose voices once sang with us here,
But to-day are swelling the chorus up there!
Who can tell how they hover on golden wing,
To list' to the carols that they used to sing?

These notes have outlived all the changes of time,
Increasing in volume and music sublime;
And to-day o'er the wide world a multitude throng
Are singing again that most beautiful song.
Will it ever be hushed?   Ah, never, no never!
Glory to God! we will sing it forever.

'T .vas good-will and peace.   What a beautiful thought
The Babe in the manger at Bethlehem brought!
Precious motto of love! let us make it ours;
'Twill make this rough world a garden of flowers.
Let us live it and sing it wherever we rove,
'Till we spend Chrismas-day with Jesus above.

THE BABY OF BETHLEHEM.

Christmas, 1882.

ALL hail to the day through eternity blest,
The day to the children the brightest and best;
Of all days in the year the happiest to them —
Birthday of the Baby of Bethlehem.

There are many fair sights in this world of toil,
But oh, none are so sweet as an infant's smile!
How I'd like to have seen that beautiful gem,
The smile of the Baby of Bethlehem!

The angels beheld it and came down to sing,
Glad tidings of joy to all people we bring;
Good-will and peace sang the heavenly throng—
'Twas the Baby made that beautiful song.

Then from out the blue sky there came a bright star,
Which the sages beheld and followed afar;
'Twas the Baby's star, and in safety it led
Their feet all the way to his manger bed.

That song sung by angelic choristers then
Is sung ever since by the children of men;
Sang on earth to-day, old and young will unite,
And sung up in Heaven by the robed in white.

Ah, how many dear children we loved are gone,
And are singing to-day by the golden throne!
Some sang good-will and peace upon earth last year,
But now they are swelling the chorus up there.

Come children and join in the beautiful strains
That were sung by the angels first on the plains,
And give each little heart to shine as a gem
In the crown of the Baby of Bethlehem.

FAREWELL OLD YEAR.

FAREWELL old year
With all thy care,
With all thy load of good and ill.
Thousands have gone
Since thy first dawn.
What tongues are silent, hands are still!

Is there not one,
Near the white throne,
Recording angel noting down?
Can aught pass by
His searching eye?
Are all things by him clearly known?

Counts he the tears,
The mother's tears,
O'er little baby faces shed--
The golden heads
In cradle beds,
Her precious darlings cold and dead?

Tells he the feet,
The merry feet
That used to play around our door?
Now 'neath the hill,
Icy and still,
They'll come to disturb nevermore.

Does he note down
When mother's gone,
Tired hands folded across her breast?
When life's wheels stop,
And fathers drop,
And laid 'neath the willows to rest

Marks he the heads,
The snow-white heads,
Under the coffin-lids sleeping?
Loved grandpas there,
And grandmas dear—
Oh say, has he them in his keeping?

Notes he the young,
The weak and strong
The scythe of death this year cut down?
Ah yes; he knows,
All, all he knows.
Oh, blessed truth, all things are known!

He never sleeps,
But watch still keeps.
Oh, think of the list in his hand!
Too high I find
For human mind
Are thoughts like that.   In awe I stand.

But some are glad;
All are not sad;
There's sunshine here as well as snow;
And some have health,
And some have wealth—
Storms ofttimes bring a cheerful glow.

Our life is made
Of sun and shade,
Like April's show'ry weather;
But oh, to feel
God leads us still—
Blesses smiles and tears together!

Farewell old year,
With all thy care,
With all thy weight of weal and woe.
Come in new year,
We will not fear;
God's angel watches all below.

SPIRITISM.

"Regard not them that have familiar spirits, neither seek after wizards, to be defiled by them. I am the Lord your God." Leviticus 19:31.

I KNOW there is a spirit land
　To which the righteous go,
A holy, happy, blissful land—
　My Bible tells me so.

A land where fields are ever green,
　Flowers perennial bloom,
No care or sorrow felt or seen—
　The saints' celestial home.

A land where all is bright and fair,
　And glorious to behold;
Through pearly gates they enter there,
　And walk in streets of gold.

Our sainted mothers are up there;
　Sweet are the songs they sing;
There, too, our little darlings are,
　Cherubs on golden wing.

They hover round our pathway here;
　Our weary feet attend;

In dreams they whisper in our ear,
    And o'er our pillow bend.

But not through tables do they talk,
    Or medium's hand and pen.
Away! the sacrilegious thought,
    Offspring of foolish men!

Oh, shame upon the minds of those
    Who dare be so profane,
Names of departed souls to use
    For sake of paltry gain!

'Tis only Satan and his hosts,
    On scientific track—
Wizards, and witches, goblins, ghosts,
    At their old tricks come back.

God said, "Let such be put to death,"*
    "Thou shalt not on them wait;"†
Pollution then, their very breath;
    Their names a scorn and hate.

Long ages too the Christian world
    Fiercely against them stood,
And vengeance at their heads was hurled,
    In bonds, and fire, and blood.

---

*Leviticus 20:6, 27.
†Deut. 18:10, 11, 12; 1 Chron. 10:13

But things are greatly altered now;
   Wizards are in demand;
To royal palaces they go;
   In public halls they stand.

Our grandsires burnt the witch at stake,
   Decrepid, poor, and old;
But clever witches now can make
   A goodly pile of gold.

Then necromancers and their crimes
   Were viewed with pious dread;
'Tis "friends of progress" in our times
   Insult the sleeping dead.

If ever demons laughed 'tis now;
   They're on a vantage ground;
For rich and poor, for high and low,
   A famous trap they've found.

They used to come in black and white,
   Grim as they were able;
Now they've learned to be polite,
   And gently tip the table.

What have they done to help the mind
   The ills of life to bear?
What broken spirits do they bind?
   From whose eye wipe the tear?

They turn poor silly women's brain,
  Rob weak men of their sense;
Their insane converts to maintain,
  They give the State expense.

Oh, Christian, read your Bible more;
  Cleave to the good old road;
Enter thy closet, shut the door,
  And oftener talk with God!

Live for thy Saviour here below;
  Tell sinners of his love;
Warn them to shun the abyss of woe,
  And seek the Heaven above.

THE WHISPERER.

"A froward man soweth strife; and a whisperer separateth chief friends." Proverbs 16: 28.

How I love the sayings of Solomon's times!
    I learned them well in the days of my youth.
They are as dear to me as the old church chimes,
    And I know they ring from the belfry of truth.
But these notes are sad, and they fall on my ears
Like a wail of anguish, of sadness, and tears.

They tell of a friendship no tempest could shake;
    Of ties that no earthly affliction could part;
Of a bond that no court in the world could break,
    And a love that is stamped upon tender heart;
Of a cord there's no power on earth can dissever,
By the word of the whisperer, parted forever.

They point to a home once an Eden's bower,
    Resounding with voices full of joyous glee,
All fragrant with many a cherished flower,
    As happy and sweet as man's home can e'er be.
Now wretched and withered, all loveliness gone,
By a word from the whisperer's poisonous tongue.

They tell of hopes blighted, and blots on good name;
    Of fond ones slighted, and souls left to mourn;

Of dark heads turned gray, and bright eyes wept dim,.
    And of bliss departed that can ne'er return.
Alas! pure lives are wrecked, and true hearts are.
    broken,
By a word that the whisperer's tongue hath spoken.

Oh! the whisperer's an enemy all the world o'er,
    In the school, the office, the stores, on the street;
They come to our homes and around the church door,.
    Even at prayers oft' the nuisance we meet.
There are those in the pulpit, as well as the pew,
Who know by experience what whisperers can do.

I suppose 'twill be so while the world shall endure;
    Fond hearts will be broken, and lives be made sad.
But there's golden bells on the other shore,
    The sweetest of chimes that shall ring full and glad;.
And all over Heaven these notes shall be heard,
There's no whisperer found in this beautiful world.

HE COUNTETH MY STEPS.

Doth not he see my ways, and count all my steps?

HE counted my steps in my childhood's day,
And my little feet led in wisdom's way.
He counted my steps in the days of youth,
And taught me to walk in the paths of truth.

He counted my steps in maturer years,
Steps lit up with smiles, and steps wet with tears,
Steps of affliction, steps in sorrow's dark day,
Steps of anguish and pain o'er a thorny way,

Steps of prosperity, steps to get wealth,
Steps of adversity and failing health,
Steps of pleasure and peaceful joys,
Steps of trouble amid bustle and noise.

He counted my steps in the midst of my cares,
The steps of anxiety, of toil, and of fears;
He counts my steps now the day is declining;
He knows I must walk on his arm reclining.

He will count my steps all the way I shall go
When my feet are feeble and the steps are slow;
He knoweth my way; He will leave me never,
'Till I step thro' the gateway of rest forever.

THE HOUSE OF PRAYER.

" My house shall be called the house of prayer." Mark 11: 17.

My house shall be called the house of prayer;
Then why do ye bring your merchandise there?
Have ye not places for traffic and trade,
That a business mart of my house is made?

My house shall be called the house of prayer;
Then why do you bring your worldliness there?
Ye lovers of mammon in saintly attire,
Approach not mine altar with unholy fire.

My house shall be called the house of prayer;
Then why do ye bring your thoughtlessness there?
Foolish jesting and levity's out of place
In the hallow'd halls of the temple of grace.

My house shall be called the house of prayer;
I will bless the true humble worshiper there;
But he who would have a sweet foretaste of rest
Must let love and good-will abide in his breast.

My house shall be called the house of prayer;
The rich and the poor shall be equal there;
To the lonely and contrite I'll grace impart,
And bind up the wounds of the broken in heart.

My house shall be called the house of prayer;
They shall gain new strength who wait on me there;
Drink water of life from the o'erflowing well,
And with glad songs of joy their voices shall swell.

My house shall be called the house of prayer,
And 'tis Heaven's own light beams softly there;
If my people would dwell altogether in love,
'Twould be more like the beautiful temple above.

WOE TO THEM THAT ARE AT EASE IN ZION.

Amos 6 : 1.

Oh, woe to them who sit at ease
    On Zion's sacred floor,
Who spend their time just as they please
    Within the holy door!

Oh, woe to them who bear the name
    Of Zion's heavenly King,
Yet never strive to spread his fame,
    Or subjects to him bring!

Oh, woe to them who read and pray,
   And to the temple come,
Yet care not for the souls who stray,
   Nor lead a wanderer home !

Oh, woe to them who dwell at ease,
   And Satan's flag unfurled !
Yes; woe to them; such saints as these
   Will ne'er. convert the world.

Ne'er since he went to Eden's bowers
   Has Satan harder tried
Than in these later days of ours
   To buise the Crucified.

He's hard at work; while Christians sleep,
   Full well he bides his time;
O'er lazy Christians angels weep
   In yonder blissful clime.

Then rouse thee, Christian; up, awake !
   The love of ease cast down,
Or other hands the prize will take,
   Another wear thy crown.

Sleep not in Zion's sacred halls,
   But labor for thy rest;
Gather within her peaceful walls
   The weary and unblest.

7

So shalt thou sinners bring to God,
Who now as outcasts roam;
Blessings shall cheer thee on thy road,
And Heaven shall be thy home.

———

HE LEADETH ME.

HE leadeth me. Ah! can it be?
What! lead a worthless worm like me?
Oh wondrous love!
He leadeth me where fields are green,
Where flowers of every hue are seen.
Oh wondrous love!

He leads me when the dark clouds shade,
And tempests burst above my head.
Oh wondrous love!
He leads me when the floods are deep,
And every step I stop to weep.
Oh wondrous love!

He leads me when the billows roll,
And threaten to o'erwhelm my soul.
Oh wondrous love!

He leads me when I cannot see,
Tho' dark as night my path may be.
    Oh wondrous love!

He'll lead me every step I'll go,
When feet are weak, and steps are slow.
    Oh wondrous love!
He'll lead me down to Jordan's river,
Then take me home to rest forever.
    Oh wondrous love!

———

TRUST IN THE LORD.

Proverbs 3 : 5.

TRUST in the Lord—
Trust says his word;
Trust not sometimes—
Trust him all times.
Trust him thy care;
Trust and not fear.
Trust him for bread,
Trust and be fed.
Trust him thy woes—

Trust him, he knows.
Trust him all day,
Trust all the way;
Trust in the light;
Trust in the night,
Trust in the storm—
Trust, 'twill not harm.
Trust in the dark—
Trust him, he'll hark.
Trust in distress;
Trust him, he'll bless.
Trust when earth's blank—
Trust in his bank.
Trust mid earth's din,
Trust all to him.
Trust 'mid earth's strife;
Trust him thy life.
Trust thy last breath;
Trust him in death.

OLD LADIES' GATHERINGS,
BIRTHDAY FESTIVALS,
AND
DEATHS.

—

OUR OLD HYMNS.

BIRTHDAY GATHERINGS OF OLD LADIES.

THERE is something sacred in the gathering together of aged pilgrims to celebrate a birthday. Sitting amid the beautiful flowers with which the children and grandchildren have tastefully decorated the parlors and the table for the dear grandma's party, and viewing the many tokens of affection presented on such occasions, making the heart of the recipient to feel that her cup is full and running over with love; the lingering awhile about the mile-stone that tells the distance already traveled, and the uncertainty of meeting with another before the end of the journey,—give rise to emotions that must be felt to be understood. At such times too the thoughts of the heart will turn back to the scenes of by-gone years, old places, old faces of dear ones absent, and loved ones laid away to sleep under the clods of the valley, or beneath the flowers on the mountain-top; and the sigh will rise, and the tear will fall. But just then there comes a gentle whisper from the unseen though ever-present Friend: "Let not your heart be troubled, in my Father's house are many mansions." Ah! then the eye of faith looks up and catches a glimpse of the beautiful land where the loved ones dwell, and where Jesus stands ready to welcome his weary ones home to eternal rest. Again he whispers, " Come unto me and I will give you rest." Sweet thoughts, sweet words to those whose feet are weary, who are just down by the river-side, only waiting for the crossing over. Oh, how it comforts us! And, though the shadows of the closing day are deepening around us, we are able to say, The evening-time is light. And we part with the bright prospect of by and by meeting each other, and the beloved lady whose birthday we have celebrated, in one of those mansions where the Lamb that is in the midst of the throne shall feed us, and shall lead us to living fountains of water, and God shall wipe away all tears from our eyes.

BIRTHDAY CELEBRATION.

UNITED AGES OF ELDERLY LADIES PRESENT, ONE THOUSAND YEARS.

To MRS. MOSES, aged 80 years.

DEAR sister, we meet your birthday to greet,
Our hearts full of thoughts that are tender and sweet;
We have pass'd our spring, summer, and autumn hours,
But our winter's day is still fragrant with flowers.

Life's morn with its joys, and noon with its cares,
Its afternoon partings, its sorrows and tears,
Sunlight and shades, many a conflict and fight,
But 'tis evening now, and at eve it is light.

We bless and adore the great Father in Heaven
For the long useful life to you he has given;
You've sown o'er your pathway seeds of kindness and
    love,
Precious grain you shall reap in the harvest above.

Jesus holds in his hand a beautiful crown
For our dear Sister Moses, when her work is done,
Richly studded with jewels, and gems all aglow,
Forever to shine on her glorified brow.

There are loved ones now watching close down by the
    stream
For her golden sunset, with its radiant beam;
And still they will watch 'til it gently goes down,
Then they'll welcome its rise in their own sweet home.

We are passing away, and it will not be long
Ere we'll go one by one to the white-robed throng;
Let those who shall first the river cross o'er
Welcome the rest to the beautiful shore.

Fruit Vale, March 30, 1880.

BIRTHDAY CELEBRATION.

UNITED AGES OF ELDERLY LADIES PRESENT, EIGHT HUNDRED YEARS.

To MRS. WALKINGTON, aged 74 years.

DEAR sister, we are glad to greet you to-day;
    These gatherings to us are dear,
Although they remind us we're passing away,
    And nearing the home "over there."

We bless with you the kind Father in Heaven
  Who has gently guided your way,
And beyond the time which to man is given,
  In his love permits you to stay.

When you gave him your heart, the world looked bright,
  And your skies were serene and blue;
And in gloomy days, or in sorrowful night,
  He has never forsaken you.

Now he blesses your age with comfort and peace,
  And he fills your heart with his love,
And gives you a title to a mansion of bliss
  In his kingdom of glory above.

There are dear ones there who have passed on before,
  And left you a mourner below;
You will meet them again on the golden shore,
  The loved of the long, long ago.

There's a beautiful group just down by the stream;
  They are watching your sunset sky
For the purple and gold of each fading beam
  That shall rise in the sweet "by and by."

And your Julia is there near the gates of pearl,
  Pure as her robe of spotless white;
She is waiting for you, that beautiful girl,
  In the rest of the saints in light.

The Master is there with your crown in his hand,
   Richly studded with gems so rare;
When you pass through the gates of the better land,
   'Twill be yours forever to wear.

Oh, how sweet to look back on a well-spent life,
   As the end of your days draws nigh !
To have sown good seeds in this region of strife,
   And gather the harvest on high.

God bless Sister Walkington's closing years
   With his choicest blessings of love.
We will meet by and by, free from sorrow and tears,
   In her beautiful home above.

Alameda, July 12, 1881.

BIRTHDAY CELEBRATION.

UNITED AGES OF ELDERLY LADIES PRESENT, ONE THOUSAND AND FIFTY-THREE YEARS.

To MRS. GERALD, aged 75 years.

DEAR sister, with pleasure we greet you here
Upon this first day of your life's new year;
Many happy returns we hope will come
Ere you leave for your bright and better home.

These mile-stones remind us we're getting old,
And drawing near to the city of gold;
Well, the greatest part of the journey's done;
Soon battle will cease and vict'ry be won.

'Tis pleasant to walk by the river-side,
And watch the swell of the evening-tide;
And how lovely the scene that meets the eye
In the purple glow of the sunset sky.

But brighter far are the glorious rays
That shine forth on the Christian's closing days,
When life's sun goes down over Jordan's stream,
Lighting the waters with its golden beam.

Dear Sister Gerald, your sun has shone bright
Through life's long day; now at eve it is light,
With Jesus to lead each step of the way,
And dear ones to comfort you every day.

How sweet to sit down in life's evening shade
Close by the river and not be afraid,
To quietly wait just down on the strand
All ready to cross to the better land.

Jesus stands holding a beautiful crown
To place on your brow when your work is done,
And your loved ones wait in the white-robed throng
To welcome you home with music and song.

In your blissful home by the crystal sea,
Close by the shade of life's beautiful tree,
We'll meet by and by each other to greet,
And talk of the mile-stones we used to meet.

God bless our sister, and her dear ones here;
Make the rest of her days still bright and clear;
And when time shall have brought her life to a close,
Calm be her slumber, and sweet her repose.

A TRIBUTE OF LOVE.

To the memory of MRS. M. GERALD, who died March 10, 1882. From the aged friends
who celebrated her birthday for a few years past.

FAREWELL, gentle sister, we bid thee adieu;
We will not forget our last gathering with you.
We hoped to have many returns of the day,
But there came a soft whisper, " She's passing away."

We're glad that we met on the brink of the stream,
For the waters were bright with thy sunset beam;
But the same soft whisper came over the strand,
" She's only a step from the beautiful land."

The cold river to her was not deep or wide,
For the Saviour lifted her over the tide.
He has given the robe, the palm, and the crown,
And the loved ones have sung her a welcome home.

'Twas a farewell meeting, that gathering of ours
Around the last mile-stone, all blooming with flowers.
We tried to describe it; 'twas sweet to us here,
But oh ! who can picture the reception there ?

Our dear Sister Gerald, the first of our band,
The Master has called to the heavenly land.
For thee we'll not sorrow, tho' the tears will come;
It may be to-morrow we'll meet thee at home.

But we pray for the mourners—to her so dear—
For they'll miss her sweet smile in the home down
    here.
Oh, comfort them, Saviour, and lead them in love,
An unbroken circle to meet her above.

Farewell, gentle sister, thy journey is o'er,
Only a little while passed on before.
We'll walk with thee soon on the banks of the river,
And we'll ne'er part again; oh no, sister, never!

———

A TRIBUTE OF LOVE.

To the worth and graces of MRS. L. MORALEE, who died December 19, aged 60 years   From
    the ladies of the Methodist Church, Alameda.

OUR sister has gone to the land of the blest,
The beautiful land where the weary shall rest;
She has gone from suffering, sorrow, and care,
To the bosom of Him who wipes every tear.

She has left us a lesson of sweet submission,
So patient and calm in her long affliction;
Without murmuring word, thro' months of decay
She quietly waited till summoned away.

To her the dark river of death had no ill,
For Jesus was there every billow to still;
And fearless she crossed thro' the deep waters' foam,
And entered in triumph the gateway of home.

What a beautiful sight was her sunset sky!
Oh, what golden clouds passed refulgently by,
As the angels tenderly carried her o'er
To the white-robed watchers on the other shore!

We miss her sweet face in the house of prayer;
In our circle for work there's a vacant chair;
For her dear, tired hands gently folded must lie,
And her poor weary feet are laid quietly by.

We'll mourn not for her, altho' we are weeping,
Because she is under the coffin-lid sleeping;
We'll think of her now with the crown on her brow,
Arrayed in the robes that are whiter than snow.

O sister, dear sister, almost we can see
Through the vail that hides us from Heaven and thee!
We hear thy sweet voice in that multitude throng,
As they sing in full chorus the new, new song.

God comfort the mourner in the home below;
He's only a little way further to go
Ere he'll join her above in Eden's bowers,
Amid evergreen fields and fadeless flowers.

8

God bless her dear ones, and answer her prayer;
When he gathers his jewels, may they all be there
To meet her again, never more to sever,
An unbroken circle of love forever.

May our end be like hers, our sunset as bright,
With the purple and gold of Heaven's own light;
Like her be found ready when the angels come
To bear us away to the saints' happy home.

Adieu, sister dear, we will meet thee on high
When our own weary feet like thine are laid by;
We'll come the sweet songs of the blessed to swell.
'Til then, beloved sister, we bid thee farewell.

.

———

BIRTHDAY CELEBRATION.

To Mrs. Moses.

WE come to greet you, sister, sister dear,
On this first day of life's new year.
Eighty-three the mile-stone doth tell,
Eighty-three years of life spent well,

Eighty-three years cheerful and bright,
Crowned with white hairs—a sacred sight!
A winter's eve of pleasant hours,
A home made sweet with fragrant flowers!

Eighty-three years! How many a thought
The day's return to you hath brought!
Thoughts of dear ones and by-gone years,
Thoughts that are wet with loving tears,
Thoughts of your life's long busy day!
How short it looks when passed away!
Thoughts of home in Heaven so fair,
Thoughts of the rest that waits you there!

Jesus still holds the dazzling crown
We spoke of at your eightieth stone,
Studded with precious jewels fair—
New gems are added every year;
On you he will that crown bestow,
His own hand place it on your brow;
And with the saints that overcome,
You shall sit down upon his throne.

We know not all he has in store,
But those he loves shall weep no more;
No sorrow storm shall heave the breast,
For all his faithful ones shall rest.

Oh, what a crowd, enrobed in white,
Are watching for the radiant light
Of sunset clouds in your evening sky,
Passing in golden beauty by!

Since last we at a mile-stone stood,
Two of our band have crossed the flood;
They've not gone far; may we not say
They look in love on us to-day?
We almost see the gates ajar,
Left for the next to enter there.
Soon the angels again will come
Some weary feet to carry home.

God bless you, sister, all the way;
Bright be the rest of closing day.
God bless the dear ones here you love;
Bring them with you to mansions above.
And when our work on earth is done,
We'll pass the gate-way one by one,
And meet where parting's known no more,
Over on the beautiful shore.

Alameda, March 30, 1883.

IN MEMORIAM.

A little tribute of love from the ladies of the M. E. Church, of Alameda, to the memory of
Mrs. N. Moses, who died suddenly April 16, 1883.

OUR dear sister is gone; she has bid us adieu;
The bright, pearly gates she has safely passed through.
When we parted we thought the river was nigh,
But knew not we were saying our last good-bye.

How gently her sun has gone down in the sky,
As the golden clouds moved in their radiance by!
She was but a step from the beautiful shore,
When the passing breeze wafted her quietly o'er.

'Twas a blessed death, and well fitting to her,
In the midst of her friends, so tender and dear;
Her loving hands busy 'til life's latest hours,
Translated at once to celestial bowers.

We'll try not to mourn, but we must drop the tear,
When we meet at our work, o'er her vacant chair.
Her dear hands are folded; her work is all done,
Not one thing neglected—no, no, there's not one!

We sat at her eighty-third mile-stone awhile—
How lovely she was, with her sweet, pleasant smile!
'Twas a farewell meeting, that gathering of love;
Her reception was waiting in mansions above.

Around her name what fond memories cling,
So lovingly 'twined about everything.
We sigh o'er her pew in the house of prayer;
Her sweet, sacred face seemed to hallow us there.

She is gone to receive her beautiful crown,
Gone with Jesus to sit on the golden throne.
Ah yes! gone to the loved ones in the white-robed throng,
Who were watching her coming with a welcome song.

Farewell, beloved sister, we'll meet thee above,
In the saints' sweet home, in the kingdom of love.
Yes; we'll meet up there in the land of the blest,
The beautiful land where the weary shall rest.

———

THE EVENING OF LIFE.

Written for a gathering of old ladies, at the house of Mrs. A. G. Gilbert, Alameda.

WHEN we've past the mile-stone of our three score years,
   How we think of life's beaten track!
And we gaze through the crystal vail of warm tears
   That dim our eyes as we look back.

We think of our morn, with its spring-tide flowers,
   Of our noon with its busy cares,
And we feel how short were the afternoon hours,
   As the shade of the evening appears.

We remember the days in our childhood's home,
  In the dearly loved land of our birth,
And the changes we've seen since we left it to roam
  As pilgrims and strangers on earth.

Our father and mother were never so dear
  In the days of our youth and prime
As when we come down to our evening year,
  And look back on the olden time.

The scenes of the past—how the thoughts of the heart
  Will bring them all back in review!
Old places, old faces—how they cause us to start—
  The loved of the long, long ago!

Oh! there's nothing lost, nor thought, nor word, nor deed,
  But on memory's book stands clear;
And our tears fall fast as the lines we read.
  Ah, who could write the pages there?

Is it done by the hand that writes above
  In the books that lie near the throne?
And is this the record that must stand approved
  If we hear the Master's well done?

Oh! did we but think, as we journey along,
  That but once we can pass this way,
We'd have less to wish unsaid or undone
  When we reach the close of the day.

How often we wish we had scattered more love,
    More seeds of sweet sympathy sown;
We'd have·gathered more grain for the garners above,
    Had more sheaves for the harvest home.

We've sown sixty, seventy, or eighty years—
    But little more seed-time we'll see.
Now, sometimes, alone amid prayers and tears,
    We ask, What will the harvest be?

Oh Jesus, we pray, from the record in Heaven
    Blot all our mistakes out of sight.
Beneath our poor names, Oh, write down forgiven;
    In thy blood wash our garments white.

Our refuge and strength thou hast been all the way,
    Our comfort 'mid sorrow and toil,
Standing close by our side in every dark day,
    And cheering our hearts by thy smile.

And now, when the hairs of our heads are turned white,
    And our footsteps are growing slow,
And deepening shadows tell approaching night,
    Thou wilt not forsake us we know.

We are sitting down now in our evening shade,
    While the past moves quietly by;
We're nearing the Jordan, but feel not afraid;
    We'll soon cross to our rest on high.

There are beautiful groups close down on the banks,
   Parents husbands, and children come,
And our dear little babes in the shining ranks,
   All waiting to welcome us home.

A little while and our setting sun's last beam
   Will be shading the waters o'er;
But our Saviour himself will bridge the deep stream;
   We'll step upon him to the shore.

OUR GRAND OLD HYMNS.

OH sing those grand old hymns to me,
   The hymns my grandmother loved;
In the quiet eve the time shall be,
   When my heart is tenderly moved.

I see her now, with her eyes of blue,
   And her hair as white as snow,
Her large-print Bible, and hymn-book too,
   As I did in the long ago.

I can almost hear the dear old voice,
   So clear, so soft, so sweet,
As she turned the leaves and sung her choice,
   While I sat, a child, at her feet.

"Guide me, O thou Great Jehovah,
   Pilgrim through this barren land;
I am weak, but thou art mighty;
   Hold me with thy powerful hand.
     Bread of Heaven,
   Feed me till I want no more."

I remember now the peaceful brow,
   And how fast the tear-drops fell,
As she sang the last verse, in cadence low,
   Of the hymn she loved so well.

"When I tread the verge of Jordan,
   Bid my anxious fear subside;
Death of death and hell's destruction—
   Land me safe on Canaan's side.
     Songs of praises
   I will ever give to thee."

My grandma dear! More than fifty years
   She's been singing those songs of praise.
I'll hear her again where there are no tears,
   When I reach the end of my days.

They've put new tunes to the dear old hymns,
  And altered some verses I know;
But I love them best as we sang them then
  In the tunes of the long ago.

———

OUR GRAND OLD HYMNS.

OH come, sing me those grand old hymns again,
  The hymns to my mother so dear.
I shall hear her voice in the sweet refrain
  As it rose on my childhood's ear.

"Jesus, lover of my soul,
    Let me to thy bosom fly,
  While the nearer waters roll,
    While the tempest still is high,
  Hide me, O my Saviour, hide,
    Till the storm of life is past;
  Safe into the haven guide;
    Oh, receive my soul at last."

I sang that hymn as I stood at her side,
  All alone by the Jordan's stream,
When the angels came on the swelling tide
  And carried her over to Him.

Oh that sacred hour, in my girlhood's day,
　　Stamped so deep on my heart to lie,
Though many long years have passed away,
　　Is still fresh in memory's eye.

Ah, the dear old hymns! They're my precious gems,
　　The treasures of earliest years;
Set in crystal stones, are these grand old hymns,
　　All engraved with my mother's tears.

How oft' has my heart been weary and sad,
　　And no cheering ray I could see,
When one gem from my store has made my heart glad,
　　'Twas, "Rock of ages cleft for me."

Again, when my path has all dark become,
　　And the world was a winter's night,
Another could always dispel the gloom,
　　"There is a land of pure delight."

When care did its worst my spirit to grieve,
　　And there seemed a deluge to fear,
One sweet little gem could ever relieve,
　　"When I can read my title clear."

These are part of my store, but I've some more
　　Down deep on my heart engraven;
They'll go with me o'er to the shining shore,
　　And I'll take them up to Heaven.

I want you to sing these grand old hymns
    Whenever you think you can see
The angels coming on their golden wings—
    Ah yes; when they're coming for me.

Then treasure them up as your priceless gems,
    That will go with you when you die;
We'll love the memory of the dear old hymns
    For aye in the sweet by and by.

SORROWS OF THE HEART.

TRIBUTARY.

SORROWS OF THE HEART.

THE wise man has made it proverbial that by sorrow of the heart the spirit is broken, and in this changing world none are exempt from sorrow.

There are sorrows because of personal trials and afflictions. Job says, "I will speak in the anguish of my spirit, I will complain in the bitterness of my soul." "David watered his couch with his tears." Hezekiah "wept sore." Our Saviour himself was "a man of sorrows and acquainted with grief."

There are sorrows of separation when we bid adieu to dear ones, expecting to see their faces no more. Oh. how we linger over the last good-bye, and in after years how our thoughts turn back to these sad farewells, and sighs will rise, and tears will fall!

There are sorrows of sympathy, blessed sympathy. We weep with those who weep. Oh, what a world this would be without sympathy! Happy those whose hearts are full, yea, running over. Verily they shall not lose their reward.

There are sorrows of disappointment. We lay our plans,

build our airy castles, and feel confident of success until, by some sudden ruin, we are taught that "He builds too low who builds below the skies." We pursue some imaginary good until we find we are grasping at a shadow, or, if we reach it, find it is no longer desirable.

There are sorrows arising from circumstances. "Riches take to themselves wings and fly away." The poor have a hard time of it; the rich have many friends.

There are sorrows of bereavement when death enters our homes and takes from our sight the dearest object of our affection, and we go to the "grave to weep there." O sorrow, too sacred to dwell upon!

There are sorrows, too, caused often by cruel enemies or deceitful friends. Ah! who is there that has not at some time or other suffered from enmity or treachery? Ah yes! "Man is born unto trouble as the sparks fly upward." "The heart knoweth its own bitterness." Every heart has its own sorrow, something over which it loves to brood. It is, in fact, a property peculiarly its own, in which no stranger can interfere, and for which it will accept no consolation. At such times the sun is no longer bright, the fields green, nor the flowers beautiful. The very things which might have yielded the sweetest pleasure become sources of the bitterest pain, "till by sorrow of the heart the spirit is broken."

Alas! what should we do in this world of sin and sorrow if it were not for the consolations which the religion of Jesus affords? Apart from the Bible there is no remedy for sorrow, no refuge from the storm, no shelter in the hour of calamity, no prospect of final deliverance.

To the Christian it is a comfort to reflect that God sends, permits, sanctifies our trials. Even in cutting the strings which bind us to the world, withering the gourds which have afforded us a friendly shade, overflowing the structures we have reared, and disappointing the hopes we have cherished, there is kindness. He would wean us from the world. He would call us from our sorrow and its cause. He would allure us to himself, that we may prove him "the God of all consolation." No joy takes its flight from our bosom; no sorrow hovers over our head, or settles on our heart, but as God directs or permits. And the knowledge of the fact that he is arranging and controlling all, is of itself a consolation.

God knows exactly the trials we need, and he regulates them according to our strength. We should seek, then, not only composure, but submission—not only submission, but acquiescence. Do not fret. He hath done all things well; he will do all things well. Personal and domestic sorrow may come; friends depart; cherished hopes be blighted; loved ones die, while the storm still threatens and the skies grow darker. Be it so. God "rides in the whirlwind and directs the storm," or he sends them before him to prepare for the "still small voice" of comfort and love.

What a blessing it is to know that sorrow sanctified by religion will soon come to an end.   How often has the experience of the Christian been similar to that which Christ taught his disciples to expect: "Verily, verily I say unto you, ye shall weep and lament, but the world shall rejoice; and ye shall be sorrowful, but your sorrow shall be turned into joy."

Under the pressure of calamity it is delightful to the desolate heart to look to future and final repose in that beautiful world where there shall be no more suffering.   A few more rolling suns, a few more changing moons, a few more days of sadness and nights of grief, and the mourner's tears shall be dried.   Then shall ensue peace without disturbance, rest without weariness, gain without loss, sweet without bitter, pleasure without pain, joy without sorrow, life without death.

> The heart hath sorrows of its own,
> And grief to other hearts unknown;
> But One alone can it unseal, .
> And He the broken heart will heal.

HYMN.

WHEN storms are bursting o'er my head,
When on sharp thorns my feet must tread,
When sorrows deep encompass me,
And thro' the mist I cannot see,
    Let me hide, oh, let me hide,
    " Rock of ages," hide in thee!

When my heart is sad and lone,
When I mourn for loved ones gone,
When earthly comforts from me flee,
And all the world is blank to me,
    Let me hide, oh, let me hide,
    " Rock of ages," hide in thee!

When I weep o'er cradle beds,
When I miss the little heads,
When crushed with grief my soul must be,
And not one friend can comfort me,
    Let me hide, oh, let me hide,
    " Rock of ages," hide in thee!

When in darkest shades I lie,
When the Jordan's stream is nigh,
When death's angel comes for me,
And his cold, pale face I see,
    Let me hide, oh, let me hide,
    " Rock of ages," hide in thee!

HYMN.

O JESUS, let me to thee come,
While a pilgrim here I roam.
Earthly pleasures pass away;
Earthly treasures will not stay.
    Only thou my portion be;
    Nothing can I hold but thee.

Flowers o'er my pathway grow,
Fade ere I their fragrance know;
Plagues and woe around me lie;
Everything I love must die.
    Only thou my portion be;
    Nothing can I hold but thee.

Saviour, I would humbly come;
Guide me to the better home;
Teach me how I can submit,
Patient lie at thy dear feet.
    Only thou my portion be;
    Nothing can I keep but thee.

DEATH OF A BABE.

Age, ten months.

FAREWELL, my little tender flower,
   Nipped in thine opening bud.
Thou'rt gone to bloom in a heavenly bower
   In the paradise of God.

Transplanted to a better soil,
   A healthier, happier shore,
No storms thy beauty can ever spoil;
   No death shall destroy thee more.

Sweet babe, how blest a lot is thine
   Thus young from earth to go,
So soon a star in bliss to shine,
   Escaped from every woe!

Clothed in a robe of spotless white,
   Like cherub form divine,
No song more sweet, no smile more bright,
   My angel boy, than thine.

Thou'rt buried in a stranger land,
   Beneath a field of snow,
And o'er thy grave no kindred hand
   Can plant a flower to grow.

I think that I could better bear
    To lose thy little face
If I could sometimes drop a tear
    On thy cold resting-place.

But I will yield thee up in trust
    To him who doth not sleep.
Dear Father, watch the tiny dust;
    The precious relic keep.

And when the trumpet thro' the skies
    Shall call us all to stand,
Oh, let my little flower arise
    And bloom at thy right hand.

Then go, my little darling, go;
    Sing to thy Saviour's name.
'Twill not be very long, I know,
    Ere I shall do the same.

By and by I hope to join thee
    On that happy, blissful shore,
Ne'er again, dear boy, to leave thee.
    We shall meet to part no more.

Canada West, 1855.

ACROSTIC.

To THEE, sweetest babe, may rich blessings be given;
Angels watch over thee, sent down from Heaven;
Light be thy sufferings: joy thy presence attend.
Innocent little one, God be thy friend.
Encircled all round by his tenderest care,
Safe be thy journey, and bright thy career.
If dark clouds should gather, and sorrow storms fall,
Never mind, little one, God be thy all.

True it is there's a world full of trouble before thee;
High and rude blow the winds on time's boisterous sea;
Oft' the path will be dreary thro' which thou must roam.
My innocent little one, God lead thee home.
Ah yes! he will love thee, and lead thee home too.
Safe, little one, safe all the wilderness through.

Long, long be thy years, full of peace and prosperity;
Even crowned with gray hairs may that white forehead be.
Virtue guide thee thro' life; then on Jesus' soft breast,
Innocent little one, God give thee rest.

DEATH OF TALIESIN.

FAREWELL, Taliesin, we bid thee good-bye;
   We weep, but we will not deplore.
Innocent little one, gone to the sky,
   On earth we behold thee no more.

How short was thy journey, swift thy career;
   'Tis finished in childhood's hours.
This wilderness world of sorrow and care
   Was to thee a garden of flowers.

And thou, a fair bud of promise and hope,
   The pride of the circle at home,
Just nipped in thine opening—only gone up
   In a healthier climate to bloom.

Two years are gone by since I wished thee health
   And happiness, comfort and joy.
Long life and gray hairs, prosperity, wealth—
   Shall death all these wishes destroy?

Ah no, little darling, it cannot be so!
   Say, rather, that now they are given,
For bliss in its purity none can e'er know
   'Til they enter the gate of Heaven.

Thou art gone ere sorrow had clouded thy brow,
  Or tears dimm'd thy beautiful eye;
Ere trouble or care, disappointment or woe,
  Sweet little one, cost thee a sigh.

Thou wert cradled with care, watched o'er by love;
  Every wish, every want was supplied.
From a sweet home Jesus took thee above,
  An angel to shine close to his side.

For thee we mourn not, but must drop the tear
  With the loved ones—the dear ones left;
For dismal and lonely, gloomy and drear
  Is that home of thy prattle bereft.

May He who giveth and taketh away,
  To the broken spirit draw nigh,
Apply the true balm, the bleeding wound stay,
  And each bitter tear gently dry.

And when strength to the mourners too shall fail,
  And each parent in turn depart,
Oh! who can describe what joy shall prevail
  When they meet the pride of their heart?

Farewell, Taliesin, we bid thee good-bye;
  Recline now on Jesus' soft breast;
Thy journey is o'er; safe landed on high,
  Dear little darling, sweet is thy rest.

DEATH OF FRANK.

FAREWELL, little Frank, our darling boy;
   Our hearts are sad, for thou wert our joy;
But angels came and carried thee home,
   Safe, safe away from the evil to come.

We'll see thy smile on yon flowery plains,
   And hear thy voice in the infant strains,
'Mid all the sounds of the multitude throng,
   Oh! none are so sweet as the baby's song.

Adieu, beloved child, we'll meet thee above,
   In thy beautiful home of peace and love.
Thou art safe from sorrow and pain and care,
   Our dear little Frank, thou shalt welcome us there.
San Francisco, July, 1874.

DEATH OF A YOUNG LADY.

Aged eighteen.

OH, weep ye not for the early dead,
  But strew her grave with flowers;
She's gone in fairer fields to tread,
  And brighter worlds than ours.

Oh, weep ye not for the early dead;
  Fond mother, dry the tear.
She's gone to Christ, her living Head,
  In all his bliss to share.

Oh, weep ye not for the early dead;
  Father, thy gentle dove
Has to her heavenly parent fled,
  To dwell with him above.

Why should ye weep?   Ah! why inde ed?
  Is it not best to go
Ere sorrow cause the heart to bleed,
  And pleasures turn to woe?

Why should ye weep?   She's happier far
  In pure and perfect peace;
For earth, no matter where we are,
  Is but a wilderness.

Softly she leans on Jesus' breast,
  Where sorrow cannot come.
She's not a stranger, or a guest,
  But a sweet child at home.

She'll never heave the pensive sigh,
  Or shed the scalding tear;
She'll never view a darkened sky,
  Nor angry tempest fear.

She'll never be a wife of care,
  Or weep o'er infant's tomb;
But ever round her brow, so fair,
  Heaven's bridal wreath shall bloom.

Then weep ye not for the early dead;
  Go, plant the prettiest flower;
Let evergreens grow at her head,
  And make her grave a bower.

But yew and cypress keep away;
  No gloomy shade should rest
O'er those who rise to endless day,
  The young, the lovely blest.

Dear girl, a cloud of deep distress
  Has saddened every day;
But thoughts of thine unsullied bliss
  Shall chase that cloud away.

And if we weep for the early dead,
  'Twill only be tears of love;
And whene'er we look on thy quiet bed,
  We'll pray to meet above.

———

DEATH OF A FRIEND.

FAREWELL, happy spirit,
  We bid thee good-bye;
Thou'rt gone to inherit
  A mansion on high.
Thou art gone from disease,
  From sorrow and care,
To a sweet home of peace,
  To dwell ever there.

Bring thee back we would not,
  From joys so divine.
At so blessed a lot
  'Twere wrong to repine.
But we must shed the tear
  With those thou hast left,
For the little ones dear
  Of a mother bereft.

Ah yes! for they'll miss thee
    As onward they rove.
All the world is lonely
    Without thy fond love,
And home will be dreary
    Deprived of thy smile,
And life will be weary
    And sad for a while.

But the first wild throb over,
    And hushed the first grief,
Faith a light will discover—
    Hope yield a relief.
And a beautiful vision
    Shall stand to their view
Of that great transition
    That thou hast gone through.

They see bright wings flutter,
    Kind care to afford;
They hear voices utter,
    "She died in the Lord."
By Jesus commended,
    They hear the well done;
Thy labors are ended;
    Thy rest has begun.

And those sweet sounds shall rise
　On the sorrowing ear,
And that view of the skies
　The mourner shall cheer;
And tho' home is bereft,
　The mind shall be calm,
For the loved ones are left
　A soul-healing balm.

May people and pastor,
　And all thou did'st love,
At the feet of the Master
　Safe meet thee above;
Be by angels too led
　To hear the same word,
And find, blest are the dead
　Who die in the Lord.

Then adieu, gentle spirit,
　We bid thee good-bye.
Yes; go and inherit
　A mansion on high,
And erelong we will come,
　Forever to dwell
In the same peaceful home.
　Dear sister, farewell.

1856.

DEATH OF ELIZA.

Aged ten years.

SHE is gone, she is gone,
  Our darling is gone;
She has left this vain world
  For a happier one.
She is gone from disease,
  From weakness and fear,
To a sweet home of peace
  To dwell ever there.

Serene in her slumber,
  Pillowed she lay—
The angels came for her
  And bore her away.
Thus peacefully passed
  Our darling from sight,
To the home of the blest,
  The land of delight.

We sigh in deep anguish;
  Our tears trickle fast.
Ah! why did she languish
  And leave us at last?

We know she is better
   In blissful employ,
But we would have kept her,
   Our heart's dearest joy.

We will try not to mourn;
   She is happier far.
Tho' she will not return,
   We'll soon go to her.
We have laid her below
   In the cold, dark tomb,
And now, then, it must do
   To meet her at home.

We'll think of her only
   White robed above;
She is singing a holy,
   A sweet song of love;
There's a bright golden harp
   Within her hand now,
And a beautiful crown
   On her fair white brow,

And that radiant smile
   She ever shall wear—
Could we see her awhile
   We'd not bring her here.

Oh no; we'd ne'er wish
    To take her away !
In that glorious place
    We'd like her to stay.

Thousands of little buds
    Daily move up there,
Too fair for earthly fields,
    Plants of beauty rare.
Jesus, the choice one sees,
    Marks it for his own,
Then bids the passing breeze
    Waft it safely home.

FAREWELL TO CHARLIE.

Brother of ELIZA—aged six years.

FAREWELL, little Charlie,
Our dear little Charlie,
Gone away from our home, and out of our sight.
Oh how sadly we'll miss
Thy fond loving kiss,
When the dear ones at evening bid us good-night!

'Tis well, little flower,
Gone up to a bower,
A beautiful bower in the kingdom of love.
Jesus saw thee too fair
To bloom longer here,
And transplanted thee safe to his garden above.

The angels! the angels!
Our darling saw angels!
And one bright little cherub pushed all others by.
She came there, fond mother,
To take her dear brother
To the family mansion you have up on high.

O Saviour, ever kind,
Our broken spirits bind.
All bleeding and crushed at thy footstool we lie;
Our tears we must shed
For our early dead,
And there's no hand but thine the sad drops can dry.

But why do we sorrow?
We'll meet them to-morrow;
We have only a little while longer to wait.
We'll go, one by one,
Until all are gone—
And the loved gone before will keep watch at the gate.

Farewell, little Charlie,
Our dear little Charlie,
'Till our turn to cross over the river shall come.
Oh then on the billow,
Come to our pillow—
Ah yes! come, little darling, to welcome us home.
1866.

DEATH OF MAMIE.

Little MAMIE of Fruit Vale, died 1868.

FAREWELL, little Mamie.   Ah, what can we say?
Cruel death, he has taken our darling away,
One dear little face from the family throng,
And one sweet little voice from the children's song.

Our little dear Mamie, she has gone to that shore
Where she said she would never be sick any more.
Ah, how little we thought the pale messenger near
Commissioned to carry our loved one up there!

There's one less in the circle so dear to our heart,
The little twin circle—with one we must part.
There's a void in the household, and long we shall miss
The bright little smile, and the fond, loving kiss.

But oh, there's one more in that beautiful group
Of golden-winged cherubs, could we but look up
Thro' the thick crystal veil of our fast flowing tears
To the spot where our darling in radiance appears.

White-robed little songsters, hark! hark! how they sing;
With glad hallelujah's they make Heaven ring.
There's no musical strains in that beautiful land
Half so sweet as the notes of that innocent band.

Adieu, little Mamie, dear one gone out of sight;
We will come to thee soon in that world so bright.
Watch for us, darling, one by one as we come.
We may not be far from thy sweet, happy home.

Oh that Jesus, the Master, may help us to say,
The Lord he has given and taken away.
We would bless his dear name, he has smote us in love,
And pray him to guide us to meet her above.

DEATH OF A MOTHER.

OUR sister has gone to the land of the blest,
The beautiful land where the saints are at rest.
Her sun has gone down ere it reached its noon,
But she fought a good fight, and won victory soon.

Oh how hard 'twould have been from loved ones to part,
And the dear little babes so 'twined round her heart,
From husband beloved, and fond parents so dear,
From brother and sister, sweet companions here,

Had not Jesus stepped over the heart's troubled sea,
And whispered so sweetly, Leave them all to me.
She knew she could trust him, for he was her rock,
And her little darlings were lambs of his flock.

She sang of the rock that was rifted for her;
She reached one of its clefts and hid herself there,
While he made all his love and glory pass by,
And gave her a view of the mansions on high.

She beheld the redeemed in the white-robed throng
Preparing to greet her with a welcome song.
They wafted sweet music over Jordan's tide.
Oh, what a reception! with rapture she cried.

Dear friends of the loved one, oh mourn not for her,
But think of her swelling the chorus up there
Of that beautiful song which only those sing
Who wash their robes white in the blood of the King.

But she will not forget her dear ones below.
Ah no! she'll be near them wherever they go;
O'er the two little heads on their pillow she'll bend,
And with mother's fond love will their pathway attend.

O beautiful truth! death does not dissever
The soft cord of love that binds us together.
Love strengthens and grows thro' eternity's years,
And the thoughts of such bliss our pilgrimage cheers.

Our sister's not dead, tho' she sleeps in the tomb,
And over her head the sweet flowers shall bloom;
She has gone to repose on the evergreen hills,
And to drink of the streams of the crystal rills.

Bring her back we would not from those Eden bowers,
To suffering and care in this world of ours.
Ah no! sweet sister, it is well, it is well.
We bow with submission, and bid thee farewell.
March, 1882.

BABY'S DEATH.

I'VE seen an infant die—
>   Dear little one!
Closed its once sparkling eye—
>   Sweet little one!
How peacefully he'll lie—
>   Calm little one!
He never more will cry—
>   Loved little one!
Nor heave the sad, sad sigh—
>   Blest little one!
No danger e'er'll be nigh
>   Thee, little one!
In yonder world on high
>   Safe, little one!
A star above the sky
>   Shine, little one!
With cherub bands now fly—
>   Fair little one!
To meet thee I will try—
>   Bright little one!
'Til then farewell, good-bye—
>   My little one!

LINES FOR AN INFANT'S TOMB-STONE.

SLEEP, little one, sleep
 Safe, safe in the fold.
Shine, little one, shine
 . Brighter than gold.
Sing, little 'one, sing
 On thy Saviour's breast;
Sing praises to his name
 Who brought thee to rest.

———

How blest is thy lot,
Where sorrow comes not
 So early to dwell!
How sweet is thy rest
On Jesus' soft breast!
 Little darling, farewell.

A BEREAVED MOTHER.

I saw a mother prostrate in tears,
        Ah! I knew why—
Her darling child, hope of future years,
        Laid down to die.

Oh! let her weep; 'twill ease her poor heart.
        Chide her not so.
'Tis hard with little treasures to part
        All mothers know.

Weep, mother, weep; God will not chide;
        He knows thy grief.
Lie at his feet; in his love confide;
        He'll give relief.

And when the first throb is hush'd and gone,
        Then, then look up.
Thy flower is blooming by his throne—
        O precious hope!

Think of him now in that garden fair
        With a cherub band;
Live to meet him again over there
        In the better land.

·THE BRIDE.

I SAW her in her bridal dress,
  Her golden ringlet hair;
And in each soft and silken tress
  I placed a flow'ret fair.

I 'twined for her a bridal wreath,
  And placed it on her brow;
I kissed the blooming cheek beneath,
  The rosy lips below.

I saw her to the altar led
  By him who won her heart;
I stood beside her while she said,
  'Til death us two shall part.

I pressed her to my heart of love;
  I dropt the parting tear,
As from my sight I saw her move,
  Another's lot to share.

I watched the boat steam from the shore,
  Where many an hour we'd spent;
But thought not I should never more
  Walk with my lovely friend.

In six short weeks our darling one
  Was brought us home again,
To lay her in the lowly tomb;
  And all our tears were vain.

We robed her in her bridal dress;
  We curled her golden hair,
And in each soft and silken tress
  We placed a rose so fair.

We kissed again the lovely cheek,
  Now marble cold and pale;
And one stood by who could not speak
  His sad and bitter tale.

We laid her in her silent bed,
  Beneath the ground so low,
And planted at her feet and head
  Her favorite flowers to grow.

Sweet girl, we mourn thine early doom,
  But know thou'rt safe above;
And 'round thy beauteous head shall bloom
  Heaven's bridal wreath of love.

MISCELLANEOUS.

11

THE HOUSE OF GOD.

 LOVE the house of God
    Wherever it doth stand—
In city street, or country road,
    Native or foreign land.
I love the house of God
    Whate'er its walls may be—
Of marble, stone, of brick or wood—
    'Tis all the same to me.

I'd see it not too good
    If it were made of gold,
If in full splendor now it stood,
    Like Solomon's of old.
I like to hear the bell
    Sound from a lofty tower.
I like the deep-toned organ's swell—
    The Sabbath's peaceful hour.

I love the house of God;
    I'd like to see it full
Of rich and great, of wise and good,
    The bright, the beautiful.

I like the word proclaimed,
    From off the sacred stand,
By learned men for talent famed,
    The wisest in the land.

'Tis right it should be so.
    Our brightest glory's dim.
Wealth, beauty, talent He bestows—
    Then use them all for, Him.
Ye who have gold in store,
    And love your Saviour's name,
Build more of these upon your shore,
    To celebrate his fame.

I love the house of God
    That stands in olden style,
And old-style sermons, plain, good food,
    To crowds in every aisle.
Love too the good old songs
    And hymns, almost divine,
Sung out by congregated tongues;
    All in full chorus join.

I love to hear the word
    Preached with fervent zeal
By humble men who love their Lord
    And do their Master's will.

I love to see men bow
  Around the altar full,
And while contrition's tear-drops flow
  Seek mercy for their soul.

I love the house of God
  In alley, court, or lane,
Where want and toil has its abode,
  And sin and sorrow reign.
Young men, go work therein;
  Seek for the outcast poor;
Go tell them Jesus saves from sin,
  And your reward is sure.

I love the house of God
  O'er hill and valley seen,
In public walks, or private road,
  Or on the village green.
I love it in the field,
  Amid the birds and flowers;
It doth to me a foretaste yield
  Of Eden's happy bowers.

I love the house of God
  Out in the forest wild,
A little shanty made of wood
  By some lone wandering child.

Some Jacob far from home,
  And dear ones forced to part,
Finds here a ladder—angels come
  To cheer his lonely heart.

I love the house of God,
  And to it oft repair.
What could I do in life's rough road
  Without the place of prayer?
How good along the way-side
  Her quiet walls to me;
It helps to still the stormy tide
  Of time's eventful sea.

I love thy house, O God!
  Thy temple, oh, how fair!
In city street, or country road—
  I love it everywhere.
And when from earth I move
  Safe across the river,
Dear Father, to thy house above
  Take me to dwell forever.

THE LADIES' TEMPERANCE CRUSADE.

[1874.]

GOD speed the movement! Dear sisters, all hail.
You have the weapons that never can fail.
Bomb-shells and brick-bats at you may be hurl'd,
But you're moving the arm that moves the world.
Pray on, work on, and oh, weary not now,
'Til these dens of vice have had their death blow;
But go on increasing from shore to shore
'Til drinking saloons shall be known no more.

Mothers, come to the ranks; save your dear boys,
The light of your home, and your dearest joys.
Ah! many as bright, as handsome, as brave
Have been laid away in a drunkard's grave.
Thousands more dying in folly and sin,
Their senses wash'd out in brandy and gin.
Haste to the rescue, nor give the work o'er
'Til drinking saloons shall be known no more.

Think, mothers, think of your beautiful girls,
With their blooming cheeks and their ringlet curls;
Loved and lovely, would you have them become
Heart-broken and poor in a drunkard's home?

Yet many as tenderly loved as they
Lie bleeding and crush'd in such homes to-day.
Then haste to the rescue; give it not o'er
'Til drinking saloons shall be known no more.

Oh! there's tears and blood crying to Heaven,
Agonized prayers from sad hearts riven,
Weeping in cottages, mansions, and halls,
From the prisoner's cell to palace walls.
God pity the drunkard with wasted life,
His famishing babes and his weeping wife.
His sun may go down before it is noon
In crime and bloodshed, through the drinking saloon.

Oh! how can men live on traffic like this—
Tears of widows, orphans, babes in distress.
While want and disgrace is the drunkard's doom,
They live on his life-blood and rich become.
When judgment is set, and the books appear,
And their victim's names shall sound in their ear,
Ah, how they'll wish in the light of that noon
They never had kept a drinking saloon!

God speed the movement! Dear sisters, go on,
And stop not to rest 'til the work be done;
Bind up the wounds of the broken-hearted
From whom the joys of life are departed;

Once pure and happy and bright as the noon,
Their sorrows come from the drinking saloon.
Oh! go on increasing from shore to shore
'Til these dens of vice shall exist no more.

––––––

TOBACCO.

OF all the sore evils done under the sun
The use of tobacco most surely is one,
And one of the worst to get rid of, I'm sure.
Would that some one could find a radical cure.

See, grandpapa smokes in his easy arm-chair,
And papa on the sofa enjoys his cigar;
Soon ten-year-old Harry learns how to begin
To imitate both in their favorite sin.

Magistrates, counselors, lawyers, defendants,
Witnesses, juries, policemen, attendants,
Swindlers, murderers, and thieves—indeed 'tis no joke,
All are more or less slaves to the pleasures of smoke.

Generals and officers, sergeants and men,
Captains, crews, and passengers, nine out of ten—
All smoke, young and old, men of every nation,
All creeds and professions, office, and station.

The wealthy man smokes in his mansion of style,
And the humble and poor in their homes of toil.
Then the merchant, he smokes, and so does his clerk,
The men who do nothing, and men of hard work.

The great orator smokes as he studies his speech,
And the clergyman smokes before he can preach;
Our church members smoke—alas! some of them chew;
If you ask the good sexton, he'll show you their pew.

Our pulpits, our parlors, our courts, and our halls,
Our prayer-rooms and churches, dear hallow'd walls,—
All, all are polluted with this noxious weed.
Oh! when shall the world from the nuisance be freed?

I'll say nothing of bar-rooms, operas, or plays,
Of billiard saloons, of the streets and highways,
Of idlers and drunkards—who of course approve it—
But why should a Christian gentleman love it?

Does it give to the cheek a bright glow of health?
Does it fill up the pockets with needful wealth?
Does it give to the person an air more refined,
Or in any way tend to improvement of mind?

To all of these questions you must reply, No!
Then why do you love to indulge in it so?
A Christian in all things should aim to be pure,
But tobacco's no help to holiness, sure.

I beg to propose that young ladies combine
In one grand opposition movement to join;
That they sign a pledge, and henceforward declare
That no man who smokes shall their company share—

Resolv'd that wherever invited to go,
If they use tobacco, to firmly say, No!
That you'll not walk to church, nor sit in the pew
With a man whom you know will drink, smoke, or chew.

Dear girls, don't be frightened, but keep to your text,
And though for a time the beaux may be vexed,
We shall see in these days a great reformation,
And tobacco will die in the next generation.

THE PAST.

THE past, the bright, the cheerful past!
    As memory cons it o'er,
We weep for days that could not last,
    Gone to return no more.

The past, the sad, the gloomy past,
    The hours of grief and care!
Our happy days fly all too fast,
    But these are long and drear.

The past! Ah, how many a page
    Has sorrow wrote for years!
Our childhood, youth, and riper age
    Are blotted o'er with tears.

The past! Oh, how often we say,
    Could we but call it back,
And tread again life's stormy way,
    We'd take another track.

The past! Oh, how many a step
    We now would save our feet!
Those steps to airy structures steep,
    That fell before complete.

The past!   Oh, how many a word
  We now would leave unsaid!
Those hasty words that cut love's cord
  And leave the spirit dead.

The past!   Oh, how many a deed
  We now would leave undone!
Those thoughtless deeds that make hearts bleed
  And leave them cold and lone.

The past!   Ah, how many a cup
  We've drank of bitter woe,
Not knowing that we mixed it up—
  Alas! we know it now.

The past!   Oh, let us not forget
  That tho' the time has gone
We have to meet the record yet
  Before the great white throne.

The past!   Oh, our Father forgive;
  Our mistakes blot out in love;
And when this world of toil we leave,
  Take us to rest above.

EVERY-DAY SCENES.

MAN is born unto trouble, no matter what
His rank or dwelling, be it palace or cot;
He may live on the wealth his forefathers piled,
Or eat bread by the sweat of his brow from a child—
And elegant ladies in costly array
Must weep like the woman who sews by the day.

Ah yes! every heart has its burden to bear,
And sorrows sometimes too deep for a tear.
True, we hide them 'neath daily duties and toils,
And cover them over with beautiful smiles;
But still they remain all engraved on the breast
'Til we cross to the land of eternal rest.

Look at yonder poor man in the public street—
He's shabbily clothed from his head to his feet.
See how rudely he's pushed by the busy throng—
Cold looks and gruff words as he passes along.
'Tis an unemployed stranger, weary and pale,
But the crowd does not heed his pitiful tale.

There's another approaching well drest and erect—
No elbowing now; they make way with respect.
He's a wealthy man; yes, a great millionaire—
But oh envy him not, poor pilgrim of care!
A magnificent tree, well laden with fruit,
But a canker-worm gnaws unseen at the root.

And now comes a woman with hurrying tread—
She's been toiling all day with an aching head.
There are little ones home, a bright little brood;
She has left them in tears—they are crying for food.
Small pay for her work is grumblingly given—
None see her weep but the Father in Heaven.

Just by walks a lady superbly attired—
Rich in beauty and grace, beloved and admired.
Costly jewels adorn her lily white hands,
And a crowd of attendants await her commands.
Glittering diamonds sparkle upon her brow,
But the heart is bursting with anguish below.

God help the poor man as he's elbowed along,
Weary, wayworn, and faint, by the thoughtless throng.
And God help the rich when the world is a blank,
'Tho' his stores are full and his gold in the bank.
And may God help us all—whatever we are—
To lay at his feet every burden of care.

TO THE LITTLE STRANGER.

WELCOME, welcome little stranger,
  Sweetest of earthly flowers,
Safe arrived, and free from danger—
  Welcome to these hearts of ours.

Yes, welcome to our warmest love,
  Little darling baby boy;
Well-spring of pleasure thou wilt prove,
  Father's hope and mother's joy.

Lonely and dull this earth would be,
  What a sad and dreary place,
If little loved ones such as thee
  Came not here our hearts to bless.

'Tis true that care as well doth come,
  And our hands must harder toil;
But yet it is a cheerless home
  Where there is no infant's smile.

Angels, hovering o'er thy pillow,
  Guard thee as a precious gem,
While o'er every rising billow
  Shines the star of Bethlehem.

Jesus bless the little stranger,
  And strew his path with flowers,
Save from sorrow, shield from danger,
  Bless him in this world of ours.

FLIRTATION.

THE hand that plucks a lovely flower,
  Fresh as the morn of May,
Wears it upon his breast an hour,
  Then throws it far away,

May find that it has left a thorn
  Which he can ne'er extract,
When that forgotten flower is borne
  Far from his thoughtless track.

Dear Lillie was the sweetest flower
  That e'er on earth could bloom,
Fit to adorn the loveliest bower
  That man can call his home.

There came a man, a Christian man,
  Of stern integrity,
And in the church no other man
  Was thought so good as he.

He 'twined around her fresh young heart,
  He tied the lover's knot,
Then coolly cut the cords apart,
  And all his vows forgot.

Ah! then her tender soul was crush'd,
　　Tho' not a word she spoke;
And soon the gentle voice was hush'd—
　　Poor Lillie's heart was broke.

The angels came and took her home
　　To Heaven's quiet rest,
Where hypocrite can never come
　　To wound her peaceful breast.

Oh call not him a Christian man
　　Who such a deed has done!
He's but a libel on the name;
　　Religion he has none.

Nor think the deed may pass unknown,
　　Or else forgotten lie;
For He who sits upon the throne
　　Won't pass the trifler by.

Of flirting sinners, girls, take care;
　　From them your young hearts save.
Of flirting saints beware! beware!
　　See Lillie's lowly grave.

TO MY FATHER IN ENGLAND.

THOUGH far from my country, my own native home
O'er the wide world a stranger, dear father, I roam,
Over mountain and valley, 'mid sunshine and snow,
I do not forget thee. Ah no! father, no.

I can never forget thy kind, gentle smile,
When thy moments of care it was mine to beguile;
Or when, full of glee, I have sprang on thy knee
To receive the fond kiss ever ready for me.

Can I ever forget thy dark, glossy hair,
Clustering in curls o'er thy forehead so fair?
Thy bright, loving eye e'en this moment I see,
Beaming, just as it always did, kindly on me.

Long years have rolled by of sorrow and care
Since I lay on thy bosom in innocence there.
Oh, those dear happy hours of the long, long ago!
Can I ever forget them? Ah no! father, no.

Forget the soft hand that wiped the first tear?
Forget the kind voice that taught the first prayer?
Forget those who told me the way I should go?
Forget them? Ah never; no, never! oh no.

One dear honored parent has long been at rest.
I shall meet with her soon in the land of the blest.
I have treasures in Heaven, bright, spotless, and free,
And with her they will give a fond welcome to me.

Oh write to me, father, 'twill cheer my sad heart
To know in thy love I still share a part.
Oh send me a blessing, far over the sea,
For I know thou hast blessings, my father, for me.

To-day is thy birthday; thy thoughts will turn back
To the years left behind upon life's beaten track;
Thou wilt think of the loved of the long, long ago—
Shall I be forgotten? Ah no! father, no.

I have gazed on thy likeness 'til tears trickled fast,
And I mournfully sighed as I thought of the past;
I have kissed the cold cheek and inanimate brow—
I'll ne'er see thee again, dearest father, I know.

God bless thee, my father, through each future year;
May thine evening of life prove cheerful and clear;
And when time shall have brought thy career to its close,
Safe, safe be thy slumber, and sweet thy repose.

Farewell, then farewell; I will meet thee above,
In a mansion of peace, a sweet home of love.
There's no sorrow or sighing, no sadness or woe,
And we'll ne'er part again.   Ah no! father, no.

Pennsylvania, February 13, 1857.

REMEMBRANCE.

AH yes! I remember
That sorrowful chamber—
For that was to me the first chamber of death—
Where my own dear mother,
Better friend than all other,
Breathed out on my bosom her last dying breath.

Alone in that chamber,
My arms to sustain her,
With no eye but the Master's to witness the scene,
With scarcely a quiver
She stepped o'er the river,
For the cold, chilly waters were calm and serene.

I heard the wings flutter
Of those who came for her,
The messenger angel who lifted her up;
I felt thrown around me
Strong arms to support me—
'Twas the kind arms of Jesus, my soul's only prop.

Not a word could I speak,
Not a tear on my cheek,
For the fountains of utterance all were too full;
But at last I wept freely,
And oh, how sincerely,
For the floods of deep waters broke over my soul!

I promised to meet her,
In Heaven to greet her,
And now, my dear mother, 'twont be long ere I come;
'Tis forty years to-day
Since thou wert borne away.
I am still on my journey, but soon I'll be home.

With my little ones fair,
Who with thee will appear,
Oh, what a meeting we will have over there:
And my loved ones below,
Who are all coming too,
To thy beautiful home, in thy bliss to share.

Ah yes! I remember
That sorrowful chamber,
Where we stood all alone by the Jordan's cold sea.
Long time I've been roaming,
But soon I am coming,
Coming, yes coming, soon coming, dear mother, to thee.
San Francisco, January 28, 1877.

MY COUNTRY.

My native land,
Thy much loved strand,
Where'er over earth my footsteps may roam,
To memory's eye
Will e'er be nigh--
The pleasant shores of my once happy home.

I love her hills,
I love her dales,
I love her green fields, where the daises grow;
And oft' my mind
Will look behind
To the dear old scenes of the long, long ago.

I haunt each room
Of childhood's home,
Sit down by the fireside, near the arm-chair,
See each dear face
In its old place,
And gaze 'til I feel on my cheek the tear.

I go to the church,
'Neath whose worn arch
I so often ran in life's early day;
I sit in the pew
As I used to do,
With the dearly loved ones, now passed away.

Then I softly tread
By the quiet bed
Of those who in dust are sweetly asleep;
Beneath the tree
White tombs I see,
And there I sit down to pray and to weep.

Ah yes; it is so!
And while I'm below,
Sweet home of my childhood, e'en thus will it be.
Waking or sleeping,
Joyful or weeping,
My thoughts will turn back, my country, to thee.

By night and day
For thee I'll pray,
Where'er over earth my footsteps may rove;
And when angels come
And carry me home,
I'll waft thee a blessing from Heaven above.

ACROSTIC.
[1856.]

When I look on the child whose fond mother is gone,
And left him to wander the wild world alone,
Low and softly a voice seems to rise on my ear—
'Tis an echo repeating the mother's last prayer—
Ever breathing o'er him who on earth was her joy,
Re-echoing sweetly, God bless thee, my boy!

Loved friends of the little one, lead him with care;
Ever think that around him resoundeth her prayer,
Whispered in silence, wet perhaps with a tear.
It echoed the valley; death could not destroy
So tender a prayer, God bless thee, my boy!

God bless little Walter in childhood's fair days;
Every year that he grows may he grow in His grace.
Oh, may he betimes choose wisdom and truth,
Remember and love his Creator in youth!
God be with him when cares riper years shall employ.
Echo breathe all thro' life, God bless thee, my boy!

OUR TROUBLES.

OUR troubles bind us like a cord—
And oh ! how oft' the knots are hard—
And gall, and fret, and cut us too;
We wish that we could break it throu'.
Our Father says bring them to him.
Why weep until our eyes are dim ?
He'll make the cord a silken chain,
Smoothe all the knots, and make it plain.
Yes; if we did what we are told,
He'd make each knot a link of gold.

———

ISABELLA'S BIRTHDAY.

LITTLE lively maiden,
    I will wish thee joy;
Happy little maiden,
    May no grief annoy.
Little birds are singing,
    Merry morn of May;
Pretty flowers are bringing
    Bella's natal day.

May the star of love
  Ever shine o'er thee,
And like the tender dove
  Thy gentle spirit be.
Long may gloomy care
  From thee be kept away,
And joyous many a year
  Be Bella's natal day.

May Jesus guide thy feet
  O'er every rugged hill;
When storms of sorrow beat,
  Whisper, Peace, be still.
May lovely, thornless roses,
  Along thy pathway lay,
And all that bliss composes
  Bless every natal day.

Little lively maiden,
  Once again I bless thee;
Happy little maiden,
  Every good I wish thee.
If God will guidance give,
  I need ask no more;
His tender love will live
  When natal days arc o'er.

TRUE RELIGION; WHERE IS IT?

TRUE religion!   It dwells in a heart full of love
For the Saviour of sinners, who came from above,
Always striving the path of the just to pursue,
With the meek and the lowly one ever in view.

He who has it will ever stand up for the right;
What he findeth to do he will do with his might.
He'll do good unto all, without noise or display;
Live the life of the righteous man every day.

He will lift up the fallen, no matter how low,
And sweet sympathy give to the children of woe;
Kindly he'll cheer those whose joys have departed,
And bind up the wounds of the broken-hearted.

It matters not what is his station or fame,
Nor the church book in which is written his name;
It matters not who may deride or despise;
Down deep in his heart is the pearl of great price.

True religion!   Ah, why is the jewel so rare?
Why so many false diamonds in vanity fair?
Why this glitter and glare? Oh, alas, alas
For the tinkling cymbals and sounding brass!

Oh ye who possess this beautiful gem,
Let it shine out in peace and good-will to men.
Ah yes! let it glow with devotion and love;
Its full worth you shall know in the mansions above.

———

IF WE ONLY KNEW.

AH! if we only knew
    What was in the heart
Of those who love us true,
    Friends would seldom part.

If we could only read
    Passing thoughts within,
Then fewer hearts would bleed,
    Words not cut so keen.

We meet the gloomy frown,
    Glance from angry eye,
But see not deeper down
    Love that cannot die.

And sometimes scornful sneers
    Meet and pain our sight.
Oh then what scalding tears
    Pillows wet at night!

But if the scorner's mind
   We could only know,
It may be we should find
   His the deepest woe.

How oft' we make mistakes,
   Misconstrue a word,
And deep offenses take,
   Cutting like a sword.

Like wounds from random shot,
   Sent into the air;
The sportsman meant it not,
   But it rankles there.

Oh check the hasty word;
   You may wound a friend,
And cut the silken cord
   You can never mend.

Each one too proud to stoop
   To tell the pain they feel;
The head and heart must droop—
   Only death can heal.

God help us wrath to check,
   Angry language fear,
Lest by a word we wreck
   Hearts we hold most dear.

VAIN WISHES.

I WISH I were a child again,
   To join yon little throng;
Climb up the hill, or run the plain,
   And sing a happy song.

I wish I were a child again,
   To pick the prettiest flower,
And garlands make with evergreen
   To deck a happy bower.

I wish I were a child again,
   With healthy, blooming cheek,
A rosy wreath, or daisy chain,
   Thrown round my little neck.

I wish I were a child again,
   To jump on Father's knee,
Without a sorrow, care, or pain,
   Ah! then I'd happy be.

I wish I were a child again,
   In dear old scenes to roam,
And hear my mother call my name
   In childhood's happy home.

Vain wishes all! Why wish them? Why,
    E'en if it could be so,
Bring back the loved again to die,
    The tears of the long ago?

———

THE SAILOR'S WIFE TO HER HUSBAND.

[1838.]

SAY, wilt thou remember me
While upon the billowy sea?
When thou view'st the water's foam,
Wilt thou think of me at home?

When the moon's arising beams
Tint with silver light the streams,
And calm and still the sea shall be,
Say, wilt thou remember me?

When the wind is rough and high,
When the clouds obscure the sky,
When tost upon a stormy sea,
Say, wilt thou remember me?

Time cannot alter my regard;
I ask then this for my reward.
Oft' shall rise a prayer for thee,
Say, wilt thou remember me?

Should'st thou sink beneath the wave,
And the waters prove thy grave,
I shall ne'er forgetful be,
I shall oft' remember thee.

Or should'st thou live and I be laid
Beneath the green grave's quiet shade,
Say, if there my rest shall be,
Wilt thou still remember me?

But I will hope for brighter days,
And seek Him whom the storm obeys,
Pray him to guide thee o'er the sea,
And bring thee back to home and me.

Go, then, on the mighty ocean;
Meet the waves in wild commotion;
Ride upon the stormy sea,
And while there remember me.

13

THE POOR.

"The poor is hated even of his own neighbor; but the rich hath many friends."   Proverbs
14: 20.

HERE'S another chime from the old church bells.
How true are the words the wise man tells!
The poor are hated—alas, it is so!
But the rich have friends wherever they go.

The truth of these words we every day see
Where'er in the world we happen to be;
Virtue and love in the young or the old
Go for nothing unless 'tis edged with gold.

Men will pass the poor in the open streets
As if they were but the vilest of cheats,
And think them impostors wherever found,
As if none but the rich were true and sound.

But as bad hearts beat under broadcloth sure,
Velvets, and silks, as beneath garments poor;
Meanness and lies, gilt and lettered outside,
Dishonesty covered with robes of pride.

And so it will be while time shall endure;
The poor will be hated because they're poor;
The rich will have friends, no matter how vile.
The world will bow to the wealthy man's smile.

But Oh! there's a world where distinctions cease;
For all are equal in that land of peace.
True worth is the wealth in that country fair,
And there's nothing but worth shall enter there.

LOST.

LOST, an innocent girl,
Once a precious pearl,
As pure and as white as the beautiful snow.
She fell into a pit
That was made for her feet
By a serpent, who watched the path she would go.

And then she went down—
Alas! deeper, down, down;
For no hand was stretched out to help lift her up.
No, no; 'twas down, down
'Neath the world's dark frown!
The wolf bore off his prey, and no one said, Stop!

Hark! 'tis midnight dark
By the river-side. Hark!
There's a splash, and a cry, one loud bitter wail!
She plunged in the wave
To seek rest in the grave,
And hide in deep waters her heart-broken tale.

Now they have found her,
How they crowd around her.
Cold her beautiful brow, her tresses all wet.
They wish they'd not frown'd—
Who'd have thought she'd have drown'd?
Too late now to pity; too late to regret.

And pray what of him
Who did this base thing?
Has society blotted his name out of sight?
Ah no! with our girls
He still waltzes and whirls,
And escorts them as usual to scenes of light.

But sometimes at night
There's a figure in white
That calls him by name, and stands close by his side;
And it makes him start,
Shakes his treacherous heart—
Ah, what would he give from that face could he hide!

But no; never, no!
Conscience won't let her go;
She'll follow him now all life's future to come,
And she'll meet him there
At God's wonderful bar,
Where deceivers shall meet with their righteous doom.

LITTLE TWO-YEAR-OLD.

LITTLE darling child,
   Full of spirits gay,
'Mid the flowers wild,
   'Tis thy natal day.
Eyes of violet blue,
   Curls of shining gold,
Cheeks of rosy hue,
   Little two-year-old.

Heaven bless thee, dear;
   Guide thy little feet,
Growing every year
   Firm and strong and sweet;
Ever keep in love,
   Safe within the fold;
Bless thee from above,
   Little two-year-old.

Pity cloud should cross
   Little brow so fair,
Pity storm should toss
   Little golden hair;
But it will be so
   In the days to come.
God lead safely through
   To his blessed home.

Paths of purest peace
    May thy footsteps tread;
Paths that lead to bliss,
    Dear one be thou led.
Father's treasured joy,
    Mother's choicest gold,
Bless thee, darling boy,
    Little two-year-old.

————

FLOWERS IN HEAVEN.

MAMMA, are there flowers in heaven?
    Said a little child.
Do they grow there in a garden,
    Or in meadows wild?

I think there must be flowers
    In that place so fair;
I don't see the use of bowers
    With no roses there.

Grandpa says there's one big tree
    Every month has fruit.
Don't you think that there must be
    Flowers at the foot?

Grandpa talked to me last night
    'Bout the streets of gold,
And crowds of people all in white—
    Said 'twas baby's fold.

But 'bout the flowers he did'nt know—
    Said each had a crown,
And harp to play the music too,
    Round God's golden throne.

Now I don't think I'd like to go
    Up to Heaven at all
If violets sweet would never grow,
    Nor vines upon the wall.

You said that God put them down here
    When he made the world;
Don't you think he's got them there?
    Have you never heard?

Yes; my precious darling boy,
    Blooming ever fair,
Why, we should lose a wealth of joy
    Were no flowers there.

A DREAM.

I LAID me down upon my bed,
With burdened heart and aching head;
For care had sorely pressed that day,
And I had longed to fly away
To yonder bright and peaceful shore,
Where toil and care are known no more.
And as I laid me down I wept
And prayed awhile before I slept—
When suddenly the room was light,
And I beheld an angel bright!
To me he looked like silver shining;
To me he said, Cease thy repining.
Since discontented thou art here,
I came from Heaven to take thee there.
Come now, arise at once and stand,
And go with me to the better land.
Without one word I quick rose up,
Trembling with fear, surprise, and hope.
He led the way, the door passed through,
Then took the wing and upward flew.
I followed him, tho' without wings;
My heart beat high—what mean these things?
On, on, and on, above the sphere;

We passed the moon and every star,
And soon the earth was lost to sight.
Then I beheld a glorious light;
Radiant with beams of every hue
It shone above the ether blue.
And then there came a sweet, sweet calm—
The very air seemed full of balm.
It was a quiet, perfect ease,
Without a ruffle on the breeze.
A gentle sea the prospect gave,
Without a ripple on the wave.
Mountains with golden peaks were seen,
And valleys fair, with verdure green.
I gazed in rapture as I passed,
'Til, at the pearly gates at last,
My shining guide bade me stand still
And wait to know the Master's will.
He knocked, then left me standing there—
Again took wing, I knew not where.
Ah, then my heart began to beat!
What? am I then at Heaven's gate?
Can I have passed the valley drear
Without a pang, a word, a tear?
What! crossed the dark and chilly river
And entered on the long forever,
And knew it not, and took no leave

Of all the loved ones left to grieve?
And my account! Oh! is it right?
I have not balanced every night.
Alas! there's something left undone.
How shall I stand before His throne?
Quick throbbed my heart. I shook with fear,
And cried, O Jesus, meet me here.
Just then I heard a gentle step
Approach me as I stood and wept,
And, looking up, saw one draw nigh,
And then I felt my Saviour by.
His form, his face, his smile I knew,
But can't describe him unto you.
Daughter, said he, I know thee well,
Thy patience and thy faith can tell.
I know through strange, dark roads I've led,
And dreary paths have made thee tread;
But if thou hadst me understood
Thou wouldst have known 'twas for thy good.
I know sometimes thou hast well done,
But from thy duties left out one,
And that neglecting, lost thy crown.
I've sent for thee to tell thee this,
Because thou'rt longing for thy bliss;
Wearied of earth, thou fain would'st be
In this bright world along with me.

And I am willing thou should'st come
To rest and peace in this sweet home;
But as undone this thing is now,
I'll put no crown upon thy brow,
Tho' thou mayest walk the fields of light
With me in robes of spotless white.
But I will let thee have thy choice—
Stay here and in sweet peace rejoice,
Or back to earth return again,
To suffer toil, and care, and pain,
To fight again with many a foe,
And drink up many a cup of woe ;
But midst it all this thing to do,
And do it earnest, well, and true.
If so, a crown thy head shall wear,
Studded with jewels rich and rare,
A crown where countless gems shall meet—
And thou shalt lay it at my feet.
I'll give thee too the fair white stone;
The hidden name shall be thy own ;
And thou shalt sit at my right hand,
Happiest among the happy band.
Say, daughter, which of these shall be
The lot that I shall give to thee ?
It needed not a moment's thought
For me to choose the thing I ought;

My work undone has given me pain.
O Saviour, send me back again!
I'd rather go to suffering down
Than stay in Heaven without my crown
He smiled, then said, So let it be.
Go, and all strength I'll give to thee,
And when thy work on earth is done,
I'll send again and bring thee home.
So I returned at once; I flew
In haste all down the ether blue,
Passed all that I had seen before,
And reached again my open door.
I laid me down upon my bed,
With throbbing heart and aching head,
But better rose, and wiser too,
Resolved that I this thing would do.
I found undone was written down,
And, being so, had lost my crown.
O Jesus, now the strength supply,
And keep me faithful 'til I die.

ENIGMA.

I WAS in the very first ray of light
 That came at Jehovah's command,
And I filled the world that in space stood bright,
 Fresh, and fair from its Maker's hand.

I was in the sun's first majestic rise,
 In its grandest glory arrayed,
In the purple and gold of its setting skies,
 As it glowed in the evening shade.

I was in the moonlight's silvery rays,
 And I twinkled in every star,
In those wonderful planets that roll in space,
 And shine like diamonds up there.

And when God made man from the dusty soil,
 In his own blessed image to stand,
He put me on his form, his brow, and his smile,
 Most glorious work of his hand.

And when he took Eve from out of man's side,
 And formed her in dignified grace,
And gave her to Adam, the first lovely bride,
 I shone in her innocent face.

When he planted the garden, I was there
  In every plant and bud and flower,
In every vine, with its tendrils so fair,   '
  Encircling each fragrant bower.

I was in the foliage of every tree,
  In the plumage of every bird,
In every color that the eye could see,
  And in every song that was heard;

In the roses and lilies and dahlies fine,
  The violets, and bells of blue;
Every flower that bloomed on earth was mine,
  Of every shape and tint and hue.

In the fowl of the air, the fish of the sea,
  And in every created thing;
Yes; in everything there was something of me,
  Walking, creeping, or on the wing.

I shone in that tree that stood in the midst
  Of the pleasant, flowery path,
In that wonderful fruit Eve desired to taste,
  And the tasting of which brought death.

When the first pair sinned, I hid for awhile—
  All nature was gloomy and dark;
But I came again in the first baby's smile,
  And gladdened the poor mother's heart.

When the flood came on, I went into the ark —
  In various forms was hidden there,
Safe over the waters 'mid the storm so dark,
  Till the heavens were bright and clear.

I have spread ever since, and shine to-day—
  Ah, yes; brighter by far than then.
All over the world I am holding sway,
  And sought by the children of men.

I am always seen in the baby's smile,
  In the little child's golden curls,
And dwell sometimes in the abodes of toil,
  With the bright, rosy boys and girls.

Sometimes I shine in a lady of grace,
  Dressed in fashion's superb array—
Quite as oft' perhaps in a poor girl's face,
  Clad in garments worn every day.

I'm in works of art; for wise men of skill
  Have learned how to make me themselves.
In millions of shapes, as it suits their will,
  They arrange me upon their shelves.

I'm in stone, in marble, silver and gold,
  In wood and iron, bronze and brass.
Yes; in every kind of metal I'm rolled,
  And shine in china and glass.

You'll find me in mansions, windows, and doors,
    In mirrors, mantels, painted halls,
Instruments, furniture, carpets on floors,
    And pictures hung up on the walls.

In drawings, paintings, and photograph skill,
    In music, singing, sight, and sound,
Engravings, pencilings, and prints as well,
    In precious stones and jewels found.

The forms and material in which I'm made
    Are too many by far to tell;
In paper and wax I'm sometimes displayed,
    And in books that are written well.

The rich can possess me in larger amount
    Than can the humble, toiling poor;
But I'm to the lowly of greater account,
    And nature gives me to them pure.

Sometimes I'm hid beneath rubbish and dirt—
    Choicest gems most frequently are—
Only brought to light by some loving heart,
    And made to shine out bright and clear.

Without me the world would a desert be;
    All pleasure and joy would depart;
And thoughts of Heaven were sad without me—
    There'd be nothing to cheer the heart.

But I shall be here while the world remains,
  In the fields, the birds, the flowers,
In the sun's grand beams at morn o'er the plains,
  And its gold in the evening hours;

In the spangled heavens, and silvery rays
  Of the moon in the silent night,
In the rainbow hues after stormy days,
  And the snowflakes, so soft and white.

There are those who can always see my face
  Wherever I happen to be—
There are others who never in any case
  Have an eye that will light on me.

There are some who have loved me from youth to age,
  Yes, all thro' the long, long ago,
And they talk to the children with wisdom sage
  Of my face, that they used to know.

And sometimes there are those the mount will climb
  When the pearly gates are ajar
Ah! then they behold me in thought sublime
  In the streets of gold over there.

I'll shine for aye on those evergreen hills,
  And the flowers that ever bloom,
In the white-robed crowds by the crystal rills,
  And the gems that deck every crown.
  14

But now I think I have said quite enough
  Of myself and wonderful fame.
Its surely time you should try to find out,
  And write down, if you can, my name.

I'm first in blessing, and first in Eden,
  First in Adam, and first in union;
I'm first in time, in eternity last,
  Put me together and hold me fast.

———

ADDRESS.

Go, my little book;
Go with words of love;
Tell all who in thee look
Of the home above,
Where sorrow is unknown,
Where no grief can come;
Where's no trembling fears,
Where's no bitter tears;
Where's no angry breath,
Where there is no death,
Where there is no tomb;
Where sweet flowers bloom.
Courteous reader, dear,
May we meet up there.

www.ingramcontent.com/pod-product-compliance
Lightning Source LLC
Chambersburg PA
CBHW030537040726
47497CB00008B/2491